Dedication

This book is dedicated in memory of my sister

TRACY-DAWN ODLIN
4-4-1980 – 12-12-1985

Acknowledgements

Janet and staff at Spilsby library for allowing me to use information and photographs from the Badley collection and other resources ❖ Barbara at Spilsby Theatre for her help in researching the history of the theatre ❖ Spilsby History Society members for their support and encouragement ❖ J/A International and Spilsby Lions for support in having my book published ❖ The family of the late Arthur Tayles ❖ Harriet Godfrey for allowing me to use information about her family 'The Searbys' ❖ Spilsby Royal British Legion members for use of information and photographs ❖ Mrs. Reeves [Head Teacher] for allowing and supporting me throughout this project ❖ A special big thank you to Mrs. Gay Crawford [Art Teacher] for without her help, encouragement and continuing support this book would not have been published ❖ If I have omitted anyone then I would like to say thank you to you all who have helped in any way.

Spilsby Past and Present

Kelly Odlin

Spilsby Past and Present
Copyright © 2008 by Kelly Odlin

First Published in the UK by
Paul Mould Publishing www.GetPublished.com
4 Irby Street, Boston, Lincolnshire PE21 8SA
01205 368451

In association with
Lincs Premier Book Productions: zlfdesign@yahoo.co.uk

In association with
Empire Publishing Service www.ppeps.com
P.O. Box 1344, Studio City, CA 91614-0344

A CIP Catalogue record for this book is available either from the British Library or, as below, from the US Library of Congress.

Simultaneously published in
Australia, Canada, Germany, UK, USA

Printed in Great Britain

First Printing 2008

US 13 ISBN 978-1-58690-075-5
UK 13 ISBN 978-1-904959-65-2

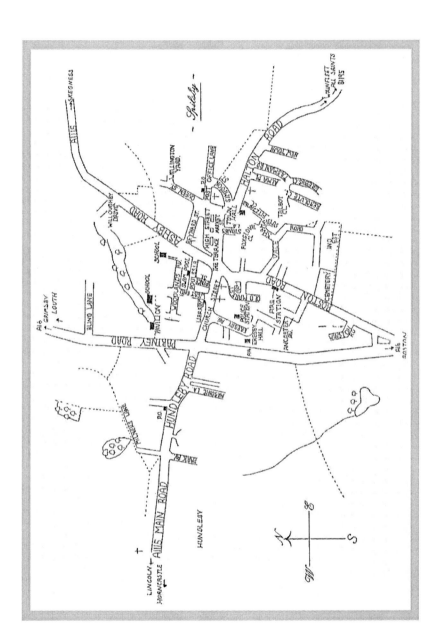

- Spilsby -

Spilsby

Spilsby is a small Lincolnshire market town with a population of 1098 [approx]. It has five public houses, four schools and four churches. Spilsby used to have a four bed cottage hospital which opened in 1902; seven years later it had an operating theatre built on. The building still stands but is now known as the Grace Swan Health Centre. Also in the upper market place stands a statue of Spilsby's most famous explorer Sir John Franklin. At Christmas time the Spilsby Lions organise a Christmas cracker day and people sing carols around the statue.

Spilsby theatre used to be the old court house and prison. An auction is held every Monday [market day] with stalls in the upper, middle and lower market places. Half day closing is on a Tuesday.

❖ Sir John Franklin ❖

1786-1847

Born High Street, Spilsby 16ᵗʰ April

1786

Education St. Ives, Huntington. Louth Grammar School

3

1800

Entered the Royal Navy

1801

Fought at the Battle of Copenhagen
H.M.S. Polyphemus

1801-1803

Midshipman in H.M.S. Investigator Surveying Australian
coast under Captain Mathew Flinders

1805

Signal Midshipman on H.M.S. Bellerophon

1814-1815

Took part in operations against New Orleans
Awarded medal, mentioned in dispatches.

1818

Lieutenant in command of H.M.S. Trent
In an attempt on the North Pole from Spitzbergen

1819-1922

Land expedition down Coppermine River
across Canada to Arctic Ocean

1823

Marriage to Eleanor Anne Porden

1824

Birth of daughter Eleanor Isabelle

1825

Death of wife Eleanor Anne

1825-1827

Second land expedition to the Arctic Ocean
down the Mackenzie River

1828

Marriage to Jane Griffin and awarded Knighthood

1837-1844

Lieutenant-Governor of Tasmania

1845

Commander of the expedition to discover the North-West
Passage on H.M.S. Ships Erebus and Terror

1847

Died on the 11th June 1847 aboard the Erebus
While beset in the ice to the North of King William
Island. All members of the expedition subsequently
perished.

❖ *Birth place of Sir John Franklin. High Street, Spilsby 1786–1847.*

❖ *His place of birth is now a bakery called The Franklin House Bakery.*

❖ *Eleanor Anne Porden*
❖ *First wife of Sir John Franklin*
❖ *Born July 14th 1795* ❖ *Died February 2nd 1825*
❖ *Eleanor married Franklin in 1823*

JANE GRIFFIN, AGED 24

❖ Jane Griffin
❖ Second wife of Sir John Franklin
❖ Born 1792 ❖ Died July 18ᵗʰ 1875
❖ Married in 1828 the same year
Franklin was awarded his Knighthood

Lord Franklin

Being homeward bound on the mighty deep,
And on my hammock I fell asleep,
I dreamd a dream and thought it true,
Concerning Franklin and his gallant crew.

With a hundred seamen he sailed away,
To the frozen ocean in the month of May,
To seek a passage around the pole,
Where we poor sailors do sometimes go.

Through cruel hardships his men were lost,
Their ship on mountains of ice was tossed,
But the Eskimo in his skin canoe,
Was the only one whoever came through.

In Baffin Bay where the whale fish blow,
The fate of Franklin no man may know,

O, the fate of Franklin no tongue can tell,
Lord Franklin there with his crew did dwell.

And now my burden, it gives me pain,
For my Lord Franklin, I would cross the main,
Ten thousand pounds would I freely give,
To learn that my husband still did live.

❖ Tennyson wrote these words for the Franklin cenotaph
in Westminster Abbey.

Not here! The white north has thy bones;
and thou heroic sailor-soul
Art passing on thine happier voyage now,
Toward no earthly pole.

Lady Franklin's Lament

My Franklin dear long has been gone,
To explore the Northern seas,
I wonder if my faithful John,
Is still battling with the breeze,
Or if e,er he will return again,
To these fond arms once more,
To heal the wounds of dearest Jane,
Whose heart is grieved full sore,
My Franklin dear though long thy stay,
Yet still my prayer shall be,
That providence may choose a way,
To guide thee safe to me.

THREE THOUSAND POUNDS,

OR, A PROPORTION THEREOF, ACCORDING TO
THE SERVICES RENDERED,

OFFERED BY LADY FRANKLIN,

To such of the Whaling Ships as shall be generously inclined to Assist the Search for
SIR JOHN FRANKLIN and his Gallant Companions.

With the view of inducing any Whaling Ships which shall resort to Davis Strait and Baffin Bay to make Special Efforts in search of the Expedition under the command of Sir John Franklin,—I hereby offer the sum of Three Thousand Pounds, (£3000) or a proportion thereof according to the services rendered, to such ship or ships as, departing from the usual Fishing Grounds, shall discover, and, if needed, afford effectual relief to the above Expedition, or to any portion of it.

It is proposed that the amount of Reward according to the efforts made and services performed, shall be determined by the following gentlemen, who have kindly consented to act as Referees, viz—

Rear-Admiral Sir FRANCIS BEAUFORT, K.C.B.,
Captain Sir W. EDWARD PARRY, R.N.,
THOMAS WARD, Esq., (Hull.)

In regard to the distribution of the sum awarded, among Owners, Captains, Officers, and Seamen, the amount to each to be adjusted in the same proportions as if similar value of produce from the Fishery had been obtained.

In the Event of more than one ship making special efforts to give succour to the Expedition, each ship is to receive its proportion of the Reward agreeably to the decision of the Referees.

The attention of Whalers disposed to aid in this service, is particularly directed to the Gulph of Boothia, within Regent Inlet, or to any of the Inlets or Channels leading out of Barrow Strait, or the sea beyond, either northward or southward, as also to any Sounds or Inlets in the North and Western Sides of Baffin Bay, above the 75th degree of latitude.

Should it be clearly proved and ascertained that any Whaler has made extraordinary efforts, or special researches in quarters remote from the ordinary Fishing Grounds, for the purpose designated, though no success may have attended their endeavours, the case of such Whaler, with a view to Reward, will be taken into favourable consideration by the Referees.

For the greater satisfaction of parties claiming Reward, the Owners and Captains shall be authorized, if they desire it, to nominate one additional Referee, who shall act and vote in all respects as the standing Referees in the special case for which they may be nominated. The Referees, being then increased to four, will, according to the usual order of business, choose for themselves a fifth, as Umpire.

❖ *This poster is the reward that Lady Franklin offered for news of her husband and crew.*

❖ An artist's impression of the home
Franklin knew in Spilsby

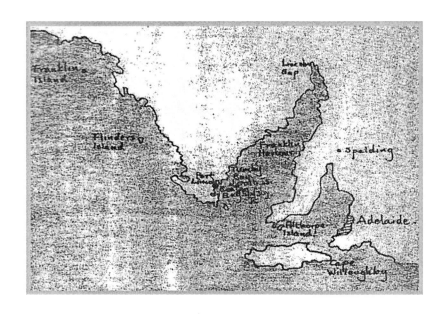

❖ This map shows the Lincolnshire place names that Franklin and his cousin Captain Matthew Flinders gave to the places they charted along the South Australia Coast.

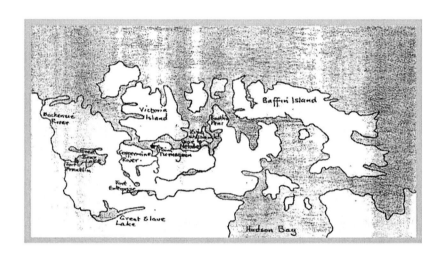

❖ *This map shows the area of the Artic that*
Franklin got to know so well.

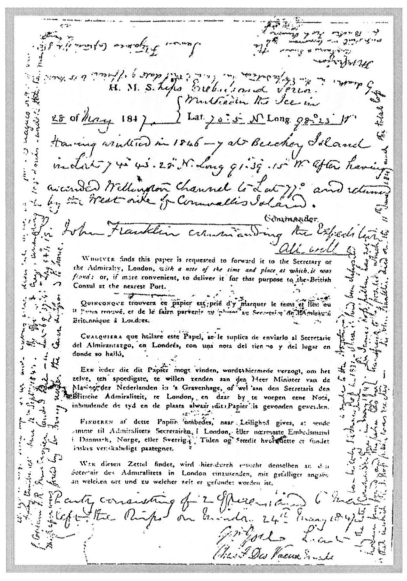

❖ *This document found in 1859 on the King William Land proves that Captain Sir John Franklin discovered the last link in the North West Passage.*

❖ Railway Station ❖
and Carriers Route

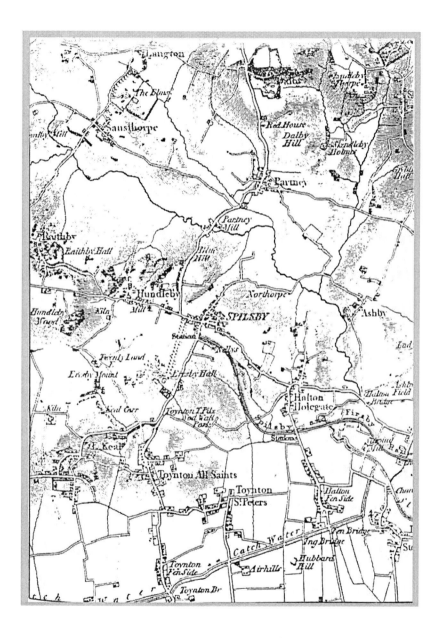

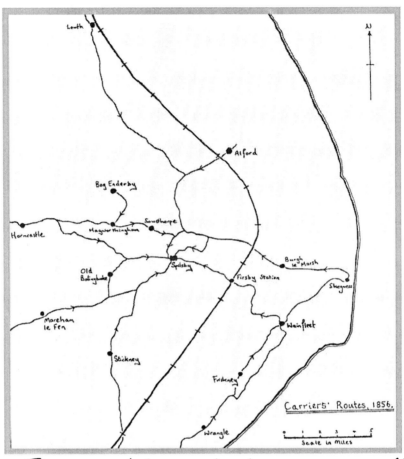

Carriers' Routes, 1856.

Scale in miles

❖ *This is a map of the route that the carriers carts would have used in 1856. In total 29 villages were within five miles of Spilsby. Carriers carts were a friendly form of early bus services. When the carriers reached Spilsby they left their carts in the yards of the inns, mostly the White Hart but sometimes the Nelson Butt and the George Hotel.*

G. N. RLY STATION. SPILSBY.

❖ In the late 1890s Spilsby was to have its own railway. It was four miles long and was connected with the main Kings Cross to Cleethorpes line at Firsby Junction.

❖ The arrival was to make a big impact on the life of the community. There were eight weekday passenger train departures from Spilsby station.

❖ Sometimes trains which arrived at Spilsby were met by a covered wagonette from the White Hart.

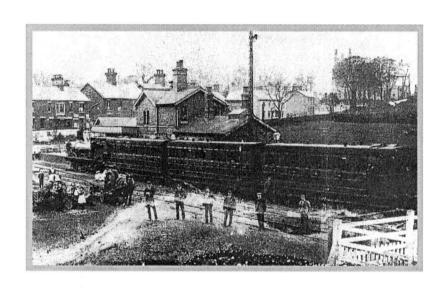

❖ *This photo shows Spilsby Railway Station with*
St. James Church in the background.

❖ Spilsby Railway Station dated 1890 (approx).

❖ This photo shows the covered wagonette from the White Hart is there to meet the trains.

❖ Public Houses ❖

The White Hart

❖ The White Hart is an ancient posting inn and stopping place for the Royal Mail. The Royal Mail used to leave London at 5.00p.m. and reach Boston by 2.00p.m. the next day. Another coach then left for Grimsby, via Spilsby and Louth. At the rear of the White Hart there are garages which used to be the stables for up to 60 horses. In 1988 during renovation work on the White Hart an old posting box was found in the wall at the front of the inn, it was dated around 1842.

❖ In 1806 the coach fare for Spilsby to London was said to have cost £2.45 inside and £1.25 outside. The Spilsby letter box was found during renovation work at the White Hart in 1988. it was dated around 1842 and is thought to be the oldest post box in the country. It was for the use of passengers on the stage coaches.

❖ The White Hart Inn looks onto the upper market place and the Sir John Franklin Monument. The hotel dates back to 1670 [approx].

❖ This is a drawing of the Georgian front door at the White Hart.

❖ And the old coach bell in the yard.

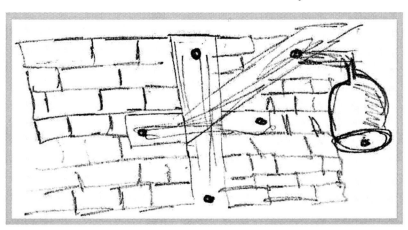

❖ In 1908 a circus visited Spilsby.

❖ Here you can see elephants and camels walking past the White Hart and Sir John Franklin Monument.

The Queens Head

❖ Now demolished, the Queens Head which was over 300 years old was once Spilsbys posting house and had stables for up to 47 horses.

The Nelson Butt

"The Nelson Butt"
Spilsby, Lincolnshire.

❖   The Nelson Butt was once used by carriers who left their carts in the rear yard. Also in 1926 [approx] the horse-drawn fire fighting appliance was kept in a building in the yard. A bell had to be rung in the yard to sound the alarm, then two horses which were kept in a field on Ashby Road had to be caught by a part-time fireman and taken to the Nelson yard where someone else took charge of them and fastened them to the appliance.

Spilsby Fire Brigade

❖ *Rear of the Nelson Butt* ❖

❖ *Spilsby fire brigade 1922.*

❖ The engine and apparatus are kept at the engine house, Nelson yard. The fire bell is attached to the engine house on the premises. To give the alarm in case of fire, the glass should be broken and the bell rung. The keys to the engine house will be found in the alarm case.

❖ The Brigade is practised four times a year in the drills as laid down by the National Fire Brigade Union. Number of firemen: Eight.

  ❖ Superintendent Mr. H. Walker Halton Road.
  ❖ Vice-Captain Mr. W.L. Dennis Church Street.

❖ A new motor fire engine and modern apparatus was purchased in 1926.

❖ *Rear yard of Nelson Butt. Former fire station.*

❖ *Dated 1896. Landlady was Mrs. Betsy Clough.*

❖ *The Nelson Butt as it looks today.*

The Shades Hotel

❖ In the late 1870s a thatched brick building was converted into a public house The Shades Hotel. This stood facing the Avenue which once led the way down to the home of Lord Willoughby De Eresby.

❖ The photo shows The Shades Hotel as it goes on the market. It was auctioned at The White Hart on April 28th 2004. The guide price was £500,000. It was bought by a local business man and is now a Chinese restaurant and hotel.

The Kings Head

❖ The old Kings Head public house built around 1700 once stood beside the parish church and was demolished in the early 1900s. It was replaced by the new Kings Head across the way from the old one [formally a house] thus making way for a new and larger cattle market between church and inn.

❖ This photo shows The Kings Head being demolished.

❖ The photo is of The Wellington, a public house that was situated in Wellington Yard just off Queen Street. The photo shows Landlord John Enderby with his wife, family and friends in 1880 [approx].

❖ In the 1850s it only sold wines and spirits and the Landlady was a widow by the name of Mary Rainey. This building survives today as a private house.

❖ Auctions ❖
Markets & Fairs

❖   *The following photos shows the horse fair. This photo shows some buildings in front of St. James Church, these were later demolished in August 1932 [approx].*

❖ In the early 1900s Spilsby used to have its own sheep market. This used to take place at the rear of the George Hotel. This photo shows how popular the market used to be.

❖ Today Spilsby still has a market, it is held on a Monday and people come from all over to visit. Stalls are set up on the lower, middle and upper market places, also in the middle market place you can visit the weekly auction where you can buy plants, vegetables, fruit and bric a brac. Sometimes you can buy a car or caravan. The weekly auction used to be run by a firm called Mackinder/Bennett and Balderston. Today it is run by Alan Cussons.

❖ Shops & Businesses ❖

❖   The following documents are receipts from different businesses in the town. They date from the late 1800s to the mid 1900s.

❖ In 1959 you could buy a new van from the local garage for £25.00 (approx).

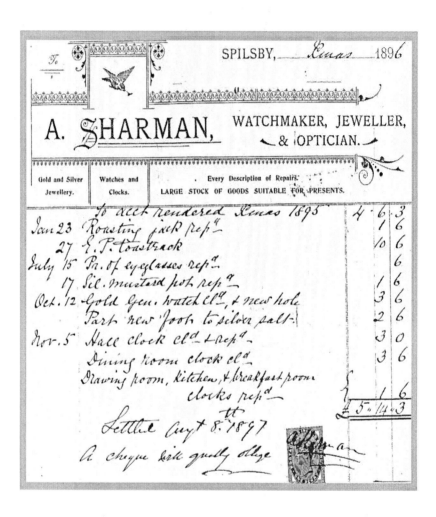

SPILSBY, _Xmas_ 1896

A. SHARMAN, WATCHMAKER, JEWELLER, & OPTICIAN.

| Gold and Silver Jewellery. | Watches and Clocks. | Every Description of Repairs. LARGE STOCK OF GOODS SUITABLE FOR PRESENTS. |

		£	s	d
	To acct rendered Xmas 1895	4	6	3
Jan 23	Roasting jack repd		1	6
27	G. P. toastrack		10	6
July 15	Pr. of eyeglasses repd			6
17	Sil. mustard pot repd		1	6
Oct. 12	Gold Gen. watch cld, & new hole		3	6
	Part new foot to silver salt		2	6
Nov. 5	Hall clock cld & repd		3	0
	Dining room clock cld		3	6
	Drawing room, kitchen, & breakfast room clocks repd		1	6
		£5	14	3

Settled Augt 8th 1897
a cheque will greatly oblige

DATE.	No. of Pkg.	DESCRIPTION OF	SENDER'S NAME.	FROM	WEIGHT.		RATE.	PAID OR	TO PAY.
					Tons. cwt. qrs. lbs.				£ s. d.
15		*hel*	×	*London*					1 1
		kair							
		Alton							

Delivery .. ..
Extra Charge for Cartage beyond the limits of the
Company's Delivery .. ..

NOTICE.

Total .. ..

Please to pay the amount above stated to the Carman, and sign his book, as he is not allowed to make any abatement, nor to leave the Goods without payment in full. Should any error be discovered, have the kindness to forward this bill to the superintendent of the Goods Department, at the above Station, who will send an explanation, and return the overcharge, in case of error; and the Company hereby give notice that they will not hold themselves responsible for any loss which may arise in consequence of the signing of the Goods by Carmgbook. It is desirable that no amount of £5 or over should be paid without obtaining a printed receipt except on the Company's proper form.

If the Goods be returned, the expense of a second delivery will be incurred.

N.B.—The Great Northern Railway Company give Public Notice as on the other side.

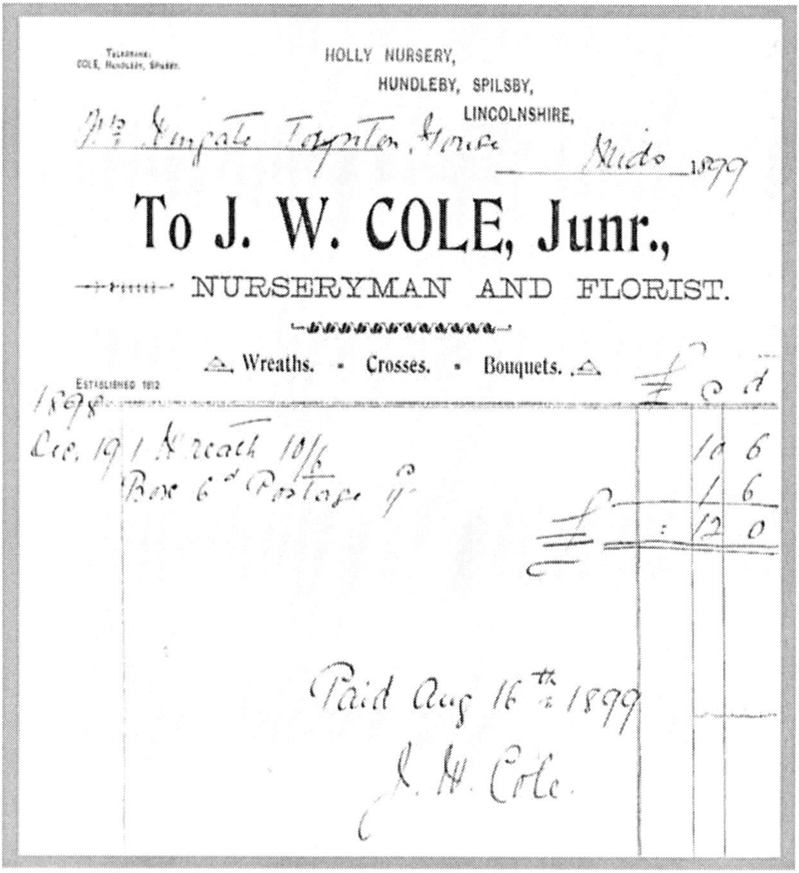

Mrs Wingate Taunton, Groves _____ *Mido* 1899

To J. W. COLE, Junr.,
NURSERYMAN AND FLORIST.

△ Wreaths. · Crosses. · Bouquets. △

ESTABLISHED 1812

		£	s	d
1898				
Dec. 19	1 Wreath 10/6		10	6
	Box 6ᵈ Postage 1/		1	6
		£	12	0

Paid Aug 16ᵗʰ 1899

J. W. Cole.

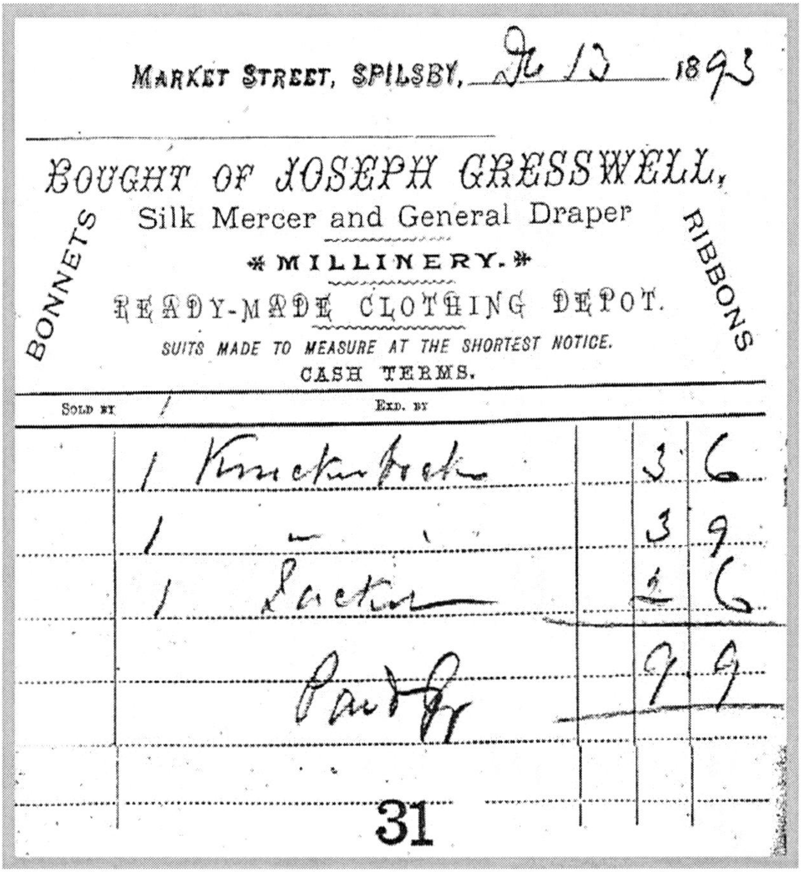

MARKET STREET, SPILSBY, _Fe 13_ 1893

BOUGHT OF JOSEPH GRESSWELL,

Silk Mercer and General Draper

❋ MILLINERY. ❋

READY-MADE CLOTHING DEPOT.

SUITS MADE TO MEASURE AT THE SHORTEST NOTICE.

CASH TERMS.

SOLD BY	EXD. BY		
1	Knickerbocker	3	6
1	—	3	9
1	Jacket	2	6
	Paid	9	9

31

SPILSBY. _June 1900 18~_

/ Bot. of J. W. GREGORY,

BAKER, CONFECTIONER, AND GROCER; CORN AND OFFAL MERCHANT.

POUND, MADEIRA, GENOA, ALMOND, AND OTHER CAKES ALWAYS IN STOCK.

BRIDE CAKES IN STOCK OR MADE TO ORDER.   HOME-MADE PORK PIES, SAUSAGES & POTTED MEAT.

HAM AND TONGUE.

Fine, Household, & Vienna
BREAD.

SOLE AGENT, SPILSBY AND DISTRICT, FOR
HOVIS BREAD
(As supplied to Her Majesty the Queen.)

Agent for
AVONCHERRA TEA.

Church Street, SPILSBY, and G.N.R. Refreshment Rooms, FIRSBY Station.

TERMS:—One, Three, and Six Months.   Five per cent. charged on overdue accounts.

			£	s	d
July	2	2 st Superfine 3/6 10 st Flour 15/- 2 st Super	1	2	4
	20	Cake 1/4 2 st Super 3/8 2 Cakes 4/-		6	
Aug	13	10 st Flour 15/- 2 st Super 3/8 2 Cakes 1/-		19	8
		2 st Super 3/8 Sep 17 1 cwt 2 st Super		7	8½
Oct	5	2 st Super 3/8 10 st Flour 15/- 2 st Super	1	2	4
		2d Cake 1/4 Nov 9 2 st Super 3/8 2 st 8d 3/8		9	1
Dec	3	10 st Flour 15/- 1 cwt Cake 1/6 2 st Super	1	0	11
	12	1 cwt Feb 6 2 st Super 3/8		4	11
			£	5 12	2½

Folio 78

Spilsby, Xmas 1900
Branch—MARKET PLACE, BURGH.

Specialities.

WIRE NAILS
PLOUGH FITTINGS
KITCHEN RANGES
BEDSTEADS, &c.

ESTABLISHED 1863.

Bot. of J. K. SPENCE,
WHOLESALE AND RETAIL
✳ IRONMONGER & TINPLATE WORKER. ✳

Accounts rendered Half yearly. Interest charged on over due accounts.

Date	Description	£	s	d
July 5	1 Galvanised Scuttle		2	6
16	Handle repd			8
Aug 2	Hire of Cycle to 16th		6	6
11	Tea Urn repd		1	3
Sep 7	Can & Burner repd		1	0
19	3 Shares		2	6
	2 Chimneys		1	0
24	Can repd 4d 26th 3 Shares R2 2/6		2	10
Oct 7	1 Brass Roasting Jack		16	0
8	2 Gallons Oil		2	0
13	Cask Oil 38 Gallons	1	18	0
18	Rake repd & New Back		3	0
29	Brush 7d 1/- each Nov 5th Scuttle 3/6		5	6
14	2 Chimneys 1/- 26th Gordon Globe 9d		1	9
Dec 8	Mincer repd 8d Can rep 4d		1	0
15	Curry Comb 6d 17th 6 Spoons 1/2		1	8
	Mat 2/10 22nd Fall Bar repd 7d		3	10
		4	11	0
	To Balance Bt of a/c rendered	15	10	10
		£20	1	10

REYNARD STREET, SPILSBY.

Xmas 188 _1901_

To F. HALL,

DRESS AND MANTLE MAKER.

	£	s	d
6½ material 3/11½ yd.	1	5	9
Dress making		8	6
Lining 3/6 Bodice lin 1/9		5	3
Prenders 8½ Steels 1/3		1	11½
Buckle Binding			9
Braid D. K. 8 Buckles 2/2	2	2	10
Sundries 1/3 Canvas 6		1	9
Satin 3/11½ Chiffon 1/6		5	5½
13 Trimming 9½ yd		10	8½
Alteration to Bodice Chiffon		1	6
✳ Bodice retrimming		2	—
Tucker & Jet Trimming		1	6½

£3 - 7 - 7

Total 3 - 7 - 7

Paid ... Thanks
1901

To J. JARVIS RAINEY,

Family, Dispensing, and Agricultural Chemist.

PAINTS, OILS, AND COLORS.   HORSE, CATTLE, AND PATENT MEDICINES.

FOL. 532.   *ACCOUNTS RENDERED HALF-YEARLY.*

July 2	Wash Leather 2/6. Tobacco 7	3	2
5	Brands Co/6. Tobacco 8	2	2
11	Tobacco 8 3 Lemon Khals 1/3	1	9½
18	Carbolic Fluid 8 Tobacco 1/-	1	8
	Tablets aperient 1/ Dipping 1/6 2 Sheep	1/	
23	3 Lemon Khals 1/4 Vinegar 1/6	2	7½
24	Linseed Oil 1/ Turpentine 4	1	4
26	Tobacco 1/ Aug 1 Tobacco 1/-	2	
Aug 1	Sublimate 8. 3 Lemon Khals 1/4	1	4½
1	Sweet Oil 4 8 Tobacco 1/-	1	4
11	Lemon Khals 4½ Tobacco 1/-	1	4½
21	Tobacco 1/ Leather 2/6	3	6
18	3 Lemon Khals 1/4 Harness Compo 1/-	2	4½
	Sand 3 3 Lemon Khals 1/3	1	4½
25	1 Syphon Soda 1/3 Tobacco 1/-	2	1
Sep 3	Curd Produce 1/ Tobacco 1/-	2	
	12 Tabs Soap 7 Capsules 7/3	4	3
	Carried forward	£2	10 7

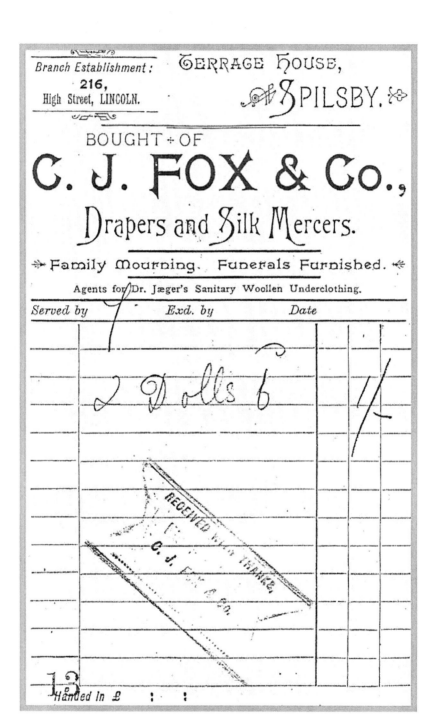

Branch Establishment:
216,
High Street, LINCOLN.

GERRAGE HOUSE,
SPILSBY.

BOUGHT ÷ OF

C. J. FOX & Co.,

Drapers and Silk Mercers.

❋ Family Mourning. Funerals Furnished. ❋

Agents for Dr. Jæger's Sanitary Woollen Underclothing.

Served by	Exd. by	Date		
2 Dolls 6				1/

RECEIVED WITH THANKS
C. J. FOX & Co.

13

Handed In £ : :

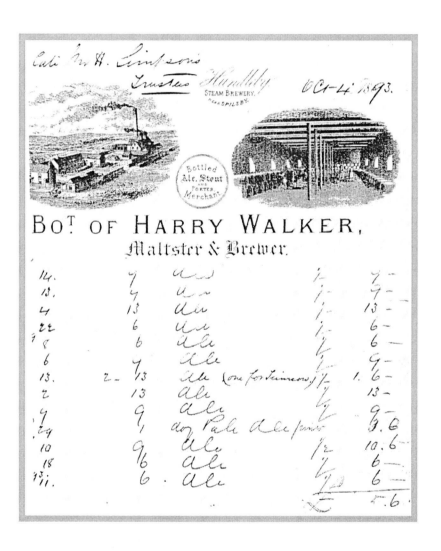

Cati Mr H. Simpson's
Trustees Hundleby
STEAM BREWERY,
NEAR SPILSBY.
OCT 4 1893.

Bottled Ale, Stout AND PORTER Merchant.

BOT OF HARRY WALKER,
Maltster & Brewer.

14.		7	Ale		7	7	—
13.		7	Ale		7	7	—
4		13	Ale		7	13	—
22		6	Ale		7	6	—
8		6	Ale		7	6	
6		7	Ale		7	9	—
13.	2 —	7 13	Ale (one for tinneows)	7	1.	6	—
2		13	Ale		7	13	—
7		9	Ale		7	9	—
24		9	doz Pale Ale pint		7	9.	6
10		9	Ale		7	10.	6
18		6	Ale		7	6	
11.		6 .	Ale		7	6	
						6	

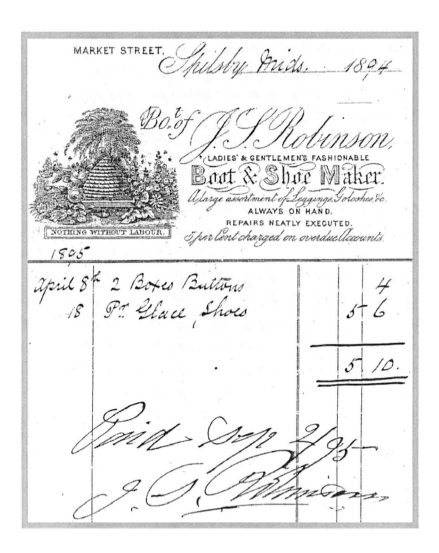

MARKET STREET, *Spilsby Mrds.* 1894

Bo.t of *J. S. Robinson,*

LADIES' & GENTLEMEN'S FASHIONABLE

Boot & Shoe Maker.

A large assortment of Leggings, Goloshes, &c.

ALWAYS ON HAND.

REPAIRS NEATLY EXECUTED.

5 per Cent charged on overdue Accounts.

NOTHING WITHOUT LABOUR.

1895

April 8th	2 Boxes Buttons		4
18	Pr. Glace Shoes	5	6
		5	10.

Paid Sep 21/95

J. S. Robinson

ENGINES
GEAR BOXES
AXLES
SPRINGS
WINDSCREENS
TYRES
ETC. ETC.

W. SPENCE

Motor Dismantler

Market Place,
SPILSBY
LINCS
Phone: 3239

MVDA
MOTOR VEHICLE DISMANTLERS' ASSOCIATION

SELECTED USED
SPARES FOR
ALL TYPES OF
MOTOR VEHICLES

Mr. S. A. Boyall, Hundleby   Aug 31 1959.

To

1 Morris Series 'Series E' Van

Reg. GUL. 398.   £25-0-0

Paid with thanks.
W Spence
(Cash Sale)

TELEPHONES SPILSBY 3145/6
Stores: SPILSBY 3269

Leslie S. Dodds (~~1936~~) Ltd 200

MOTOR ENGINEERS

AUSTIN AND ROVER MAIN DEALERS

	Cr.			Dr.		
Ford EPE 422						
Tracing and rectifying faulty starting by overhauling ignition system.						
Fitting new fan belt				1	4	-
1 Fan belt						

❖ In 1977 one of Spilsbys oldest businesses changed hands. The firm of Leslie S. Dodds was first established in 1895 in the High Street. They started out as a furnishing and general ironmonger business but with the popularity of the bicycle as a form of transport, the sale of these machines was added to the business. When the motor car became popular in Spilsby the firm built a workshop on Ashby Road 1900 [approx].

❖ As the demand for motor cars grew the firm bought the old Masonic Hall in Hundleby Road. When L.S. Dodds sold out the fourteen employees had run up a total of 300 years service between them.

GOGGLES  Accumulator

HORNS Throttlers

GONGS Sparking Plugs

VOLTMETERS Insulated Wire

REPAIRS, STORAGE & SPARE PARTS.

Pratt's Motor Car Spirit.

Carless Capel & Leonard's Petrol.

Price's Lubricants, Solidified Oils, Gas Engine Oil, &c.

De Dion Car Parts.

Peugeot Car Parts.

Minerva Motor Cycle Parts.

ACCUMULATORS CHARGED ON PREMISES.

LESLIE S. DODDS

Market Place, SPILSBY.

A Dodds advertisement from the days when De Dion car parts were in stock.

❖ The former Spilsby Manor House on the High Street. When this photo was taken it had already become a bank. This building was demolished in late 1939, in its place is a new building now occupied by the H.S.B.C. bank and the National Farmers Union.

❖ A photo of the Buttercross in the lower market place in 1860. To the left is George Enderby's house now the Tuck shop, it used to be a cobblers shop.

❖ This photo shows Spilsby post office staff in the early 1900s.

❖ This photo shows the Post office all decorated up for the Silver Jubilee Day in 1935. Its decorations won 1st prize in its section.

❖ Tradesmen ❖ and Craftsmen

❖ In the early 1900s Spilsby was beginning to lose some of its local tradesmen and craftsmen because bigger towns were supplying shops with their goods. In the mid 19th century more than 60 men and women earned a living from the boot and shoe trade but in 1900 it was said that only six shoe makers were still operating and then by 1913 there were only four. The opening of Stead and Simpson's and Hiltons Booteries a few years earlier in the 1890s marked the end of the trade in Spilsby.

❖ The candle factory on Ashby Road closed in 1910 as did the rope factory on Boston road in 1914. The Spilsby Brewery closed in 1914. Two crafts which employed large numbers of people in the town were those of the Tailor and Milliner but they started to decline in 1914 due to competition from London, Midland and Lancashire sweat shops. A local iron monger Lesley Dodds decided to go into the car trade. He sold and repaired cars and his first customer for the new motor invention was the Revd. Simpson of West Keal. In 1898.

❖ This bank note was issued by the Boston and Spilsby Bank in 1814.

❖ The Edwardian era was also the age of the Bicycle. By 1901 the sport of cycling had already taken off and a busy cycling club existed. J.K. Spence of the High Street also made his own "Eresby" bicycle. In 1903 a gentlemens cycle cost £7.00 and a ladies cost £7.10s.

❖ There were two shops that seemed to be busy during the time of horses being used and they were A. Greetham whose was a saddlers and Samuel Cossey who sold collars and harnesses. Greetham's shop was in the market place whilst Cossey's was on the High Street.

❖ This photo shows the premises of Stainton and Searby 1850 [approx]. It was a family run business. The business is now a menswear shop called Smalls, it is managed by my Dad. The house next door is no longer there but a shopping arcade is in its place. The house was also home to the Searby family.

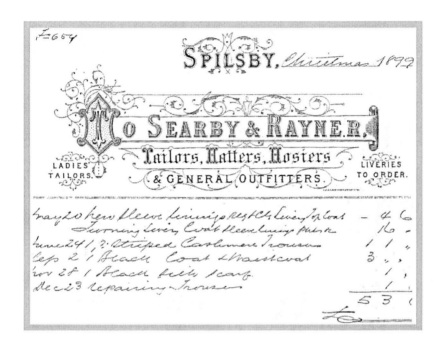

❖ The Searby family lived in Spilsby above their shop, they also lived in the house next door. They also owned a house in Halton Road and West End Villas. Relations lived in Boston Road and at the Grange at Firsby.

Searby & Rayner,
Wholesale & Family Grocers
& Provision Merchants.
Franklin Stores,
Spilsby.

Your favors are
respectfully solicited.

❖ This piece of paper is a copy of headed paper that would have been used in their shop.

The recipe given below—first casually mentioned to one or two customers —has been much appreciated, and we feel emboldened to have same printed for distribution to our customers. The recipe is a good and economical one.

APRICOT JAM.

Thoroughly wash, then soak for 48 hours 1 pound of Evaporated Apricots in 2 to 3 pints of water ; add $2\frac{1}{2}$ pounds sugar and boil for three=quarters of an hour.

This makes 5 pounds of delicious Jam.

SEARBY & RAYNER,

SPILSBY.

❖ *Also a copy of a recipe that they gave to their customers.*

The Searby Family

❖ Left to right standing James Junior, Jane [Jeanne], Arthur, A.E. Gregory. Left to right seated Leonora Ellen Eve, James Senior, Lucy [nee Parish] Searby, Catherine [Kitty] nee Searby Gregory. On knees are three boys of James Junior. Three of Kitty's children. This photo was dated 1878 [approx] as by 1888 Kitty had one more child.

❖ *This photo is of James Searby Senior.*

❖ James Searby Senior

❖ Anne Greene Sargisson,
first wife of James Searby Senior

❖ James Senior as a young man.

❖ James Junior

❖ *Arthur Searby as a baby and as a young boy.*

❖ *These two photos are of Mary Searby and her husband the Rev. William Rose.*

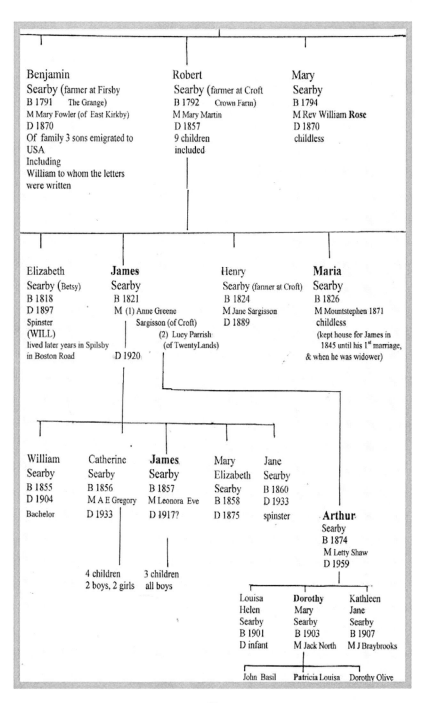

Benjamin
Searby (farmer at Firsby
B 1791   The Grange)
M Mary Fowler (of East Kirkby)
D 1870
Of family 3 sons emigrated to
USA
Including
William to whom the letters
were written

Robert
Searby (farmer at Croft
B 1792   Crown Farm)
M Mary Martin
D 1857
9 children
included

Mary
Searby
B 1794
M Rev William Rose
D 1870
childless

Elizabeth
Searby (Betsy)
B 1818
D 1897
Spinster
(WILL)
lived later years in Spilsby
in Boston Road

James
Searby
B 1821
M (1) Anne Greene
     Sargisson (of Croft)
     (2) Lucy Parrish
          (of TwentyLands)
D 1920

Henry
Searby (farmer at Croft)
B 1824
M Jane Sargisson
D 1889

Maria
Searby
B 1826
M Mountstephen 1871
childless
(kept house for James in
1845 until his 1st marriage,
& when he was widower)

William
Searby
B 1855
D 1904
Bachelor

Catherine
Searby
B 1856
M A E Gregory
D 1933

James
Searby
B 1857
M Leonora Eve
D 1917?

Mary
Elizabeth
Searby
B 1858
D 1875

Jane
Searby
B 1860
D 1933
spinster

Arthur
Searby
B 1874
M Letty Shaw
D 1959

4 children
2 boys, 2 girls

3 children
all boys

Louisa
Helen
Searby
B 1901
D infant

Dorothy
Mary
Searby
B 1903
M Jack North

Kathleen
Jane
Searby
B 1907
M J Braybrooks

John Basil   Patricia Louisa   Dorothy Olive

JAMES SEARBY Sen:

Born 29th August 1821 at Crown Farm, Croft, 2nd son and 4th child of Robert Searby and Mary (née Martin) Searby

Siblings: 7 brothers: John, Henry, Wright, Robert (died infant), Robert, William Martin; and sisters: Catherine (died aged 6), Elizabeth, Rebekah (died, drowned aged 1 year), Maria, Helen, Mary, Caroline.

Educated : Magdalen School, Wainfleet; Burgh le Marsh.

Apprenticed: Eve and Ranshaw, Louth

c1845 – 1870 Fire & Life Agent for County & Provident,Draper/Shopkeeper: Searby and Stainton, Spilsby

1870 – 1890 Searby only

1890 – 1906 Searby & Rayner

lived High Street above and between shops and had a property in Halton Road

Prior to marriage sister Maria kept house for him

Married: 1. Anne Greene Sargisson (of Croft) with whom he had four children, 2 sons, William and James, 2 daughters, Catherine (Kitty) and Jane (Jennie, later Gran)

Widowed by 1866; Maria kept house again

Married: 2. Lucy Parish (of Twentylands), one son, Arthur

At some time after retirement in 1906 went to live with daughter Kitty (now Gregory) and family in Hertfordshire.

Died: 3 months short of 100th birthday 1921

JAMES SEARBY Jun:

Born: Spilsby 1857, 2nd son, and 3rd child of James Searby Sen: and Anne (née Greene Sargisson) Searby

Siblings: 1 brother William; 3 sisters, Catherine (Kitty), Mary Elizabeth (died aged 17), Jane

Educated: Spilsby?

Lived at High Street and later at West End Villas

From c - ? in partnership with father, managing business/shops

Married: Ann, Leonora, Ellen Eve, 3 sons

In Spilsby Magazines taking an active part in Spilsby life: Football etc. c 1870s-1880s

? disappeared for 7 years and then re-appeared as if nothing had happened !

His name is not featured in Kelly's directories between 1906 and 1913

addresses in Spilsby are various in Directories

West End Villas in 1913

Moved to?

Died: 1917 ?

Descendants addresses are in Hertfordshire/Buckinghamshire/Sussex

ARTHUR JOHN SEARBY

Born: Spilsby 1874 Only Son of James Searby Sen: and Lucy Parish

Siblings: 2 older step-brothers and 2 older step-sisters (see James Junior)

Educated: Spilsby Grammar School and Bedford

Apprenticed: to father, also in Manchester and Newark

Married: Letitia (Letty) Tetlow Shaw B 1873 D 1951

3 children all girls, one Louisa Helen died infant, Dorothy Mary B1903, Kathleen Jane B1907

Lived and worked in Spilsby at first with father and brother taking control of the management in 1906

Searby & Rayner – 1921

& Lee – 1933 when the drapery side was sold to H R Small and part of business was rented to W F Goodrick & Sons

Took active part in social, sporting and cultural life especially Operatic Society

In later years was assisted in the shop by daughter Dorothy and husband

Died 1959

Name	Address	Trade/Occupation
J.E.Taylor	High Street	Fruiterer and Greengrocer
G.Temple (Miss.)	Market Place	Ladies' Hairdresser
M.Thornley	Masonic Lane	Window Cleaner
E.J.Tong	High Street	Ironmonger
Townell & Sons	Hundleby Road	Motor Engineers
A.Venables	High Street	Optician
Waite & Sons	Market Street	Grocers
H.Walker	Queen Street	Builder
J.R.Walker	Ashby Road	Plumber etc.
F.Ward	High Street	Grocer
P.F.Warren	High Street	Ironmonger
A.E.Wildman	Halton Road	Motor Engineer
E.Wilkinson	Halton Road	Insurance Agent
F.Wilkinson (Mrs.)	High Street	Confectioner
J.Willson & Sons	Ashby Road	Auctioneers
S.Winn	High Street	Fruiterer
C.A.Wood	Ashby Road	Stone Mason
E.C.Woods	Masonic Lane	Insurance Agent
W.Wright	Reynard Street	Blacksmith

Name	Address	Trade/Occupation
Anglo-American Oil	Railway Station, Boston Road	
Geo.Ashton	Wellington Lane	Carting Contractor
T.W.Ashton	Boston Road	Baker
Jn.Atkinson	Queen Street	Boot Repairer
Hy.Atkinson	'King's Head', Boston Rd.	Publican
J.A.Badley	The Terrace	Motor car garage
Baker and Webb	Ashby Road	Builders
M.Barlow (Miss.)	Cornhill	Apartments
A.Barratt (Mrs.)	Market Place	Confectioners
J.H.Barratt & Son	Boston Road	Cake, Corn, Rope and Tent Maker
Seth Barratt	Queen Street	Tailor
A.Beeton	'White Hart', High Street	Publican
H.Bird (Mrs.)	Halton Road	Grocer
Wm.Bird	Newtown	Boot Repairer
C.Brough	Halton Road	Boot & Shoe Maker
Browning & Son	Ashby Road	Stone Masons
T.Bundock	Market Place	Photographer
H.Cade	Halton Road	Butcher
J.Caldwell	Hundleby Road	Vet
E.H.Cartwright	Market Place	Dairyman
Jos.Chesterfield	High Street	Cabinet Maker
M.Clarey	Queen Street	Grazier
J.H.Clark	Queen Street	Baker
Betsy Clough (Mrs.)	'The Nelson', Market Street	Publican
T.E.Cooke	Halton Road	Draper
J.Cossey	High Street	Saddler
Wm.Cossey	Reynard Street	Fried Fish Dealer
Mary Coxton	Boston Road	Temperance Hotel
F.Delamore	Ashby Road	Blacksmith
W.L.Dennis	Church Street	Grocer
L.S.Dodds	Market Place	Motor Engineers
J.H.Driffield	Market Street	Druggist
J.Ellerby	Reynard Street	Cow Keeper
Geo.Enderby	West End Terrace	Jobbing Gardener
W.Emerson	'George Hotel', Boston Road	Publican
A.C.Farmer's Exors.	High Street	Chemist
E.Fitzgibbon	'The Shades', Hundleby Road	Publican
A.& W.Forman	Cornhill	Dentists
C.J.Fox & Co.	The Terrace	Drapers
F.Garner	High Street	Jeweller and Watch Maker
J.Gibbins	High Street	Draper
Gilliat & Hewson	High Street	Ironmongers
J.H.Goodhand	Queen Street	Painter
W.F.Goodrick	Reynard Street	Joiner and Cabinet Maker
A.Greetham	Market Street	Saddler
Gresswell and Co.	Market Street	Drapers

Name	Address	Trade/Occupation
J.W.C.Sylvester	Market Street	Jeweller
W.H.Taylor	High Street	Clothier and Outfitter
J.E.Taylor	High Street	Fishmonger
C.Townell	Reynard Street	Cycle Agent
F.W.Townell	West End Terrace	Phonograph Agent
Waite & Sons	Market Street	Grocers
D.Wakeling	High Street	Drapers
C.F.Walker	Market Street	Hairdresser
H.Walker	Halton Road	Carting Contractor
J.R.Walker	Ashby Road	Plumber and Decorator
S.Watson	Cornhill	Clothier
S.J.Ward (Mrs.)	Boston Road	Apartments
E.West (Mrs.)	Reynard Street	Shopkeeper
A.White	Halton Road	Blacksmith
Jn.Willsons	The Terrace	Auctioneers
J.Wood & Co.	Railway Station, Boston Road	Coal Merchants
E.& M.Wright (Misses)	Halton Road	Confectioners
T.Wright	Halton Road	Butcher & Potato Merchant

1937

Name	Address	Trade/Occupation
F.R.Adams	Church Street	Chemist
B.Appleby	Market Place	Fried Fish Dealer
Geo.Ashton	Simpson Street	Chimney Sweep
J.W.Atkinson	Queen Street	Boot and Shoe Repairer
W.S.Axup	Town Hall	Boot Repairer
Badley & Sons	The Terrace	Motor Car Garage
G.Badley	Cornhill	Hairdresser
Baker & Webb	Ashby Road	Builders
B.E.Balderston	Town Hall	Auctioneer
J.H.Barratt & Son	Boston Road	Coal Merchant
Geo.Bett	Halton Road	Jobbing Gardener
A.Blackburn	'Bull Hotel', Halton Road	Publican
Boston Billposting (E. Beaver)	Halton Road	
Boston Coal Co.	Railway Station, Boston Road	Coal Merchant
C.Buff	Halton Road	Insurance Agent
E.Bull (Mrs.)	Halton Road	Tobacconist
S.Bull	Halton Road	Picture Framer
T.Bundock	Market Place	Photographer
H.Cade	Halton Road	Butcher
R.W.Carr	Market Place and Halton Road	Butcher
J.Cartwright	Market Place	Greengrocer
J.H.Clark	Queen Street	Baker

Name	Address	Trade/Occupation
J.W.C.Sylvester	Market Street	Jeweller
W.H.Taylor	High Street	Clothier and Outfitter
J.E.Taylor	High Street	Fishmonger
C.Townell	Reynard Street	Cycle Agent
F.W.Townell	West End Terrace	Phonograph Agent
Waite & Sons	Market Street	Grocers
D.Wakeling	High Street	Drapers
C.F.Walker	Market Street	Hairdresser
H.Walker	Halton Road	Carting Contractor
J.R.Walker	Ashby Road	Plumber and Decorator
S.Watson	Cornhill	Clothier
S.J.Ward (Mrs.)	Boston Road	Apartments
E.West (Mrs.)	Reynard Street	Shopkeeper
A.White	Halton Road	Blacksmith
Jn.Willsons	The Terrace	Auctioneers
J.Wood & Co.	Railway Station, Boston Road	Coal Merchants
E.& M.Wright (Misses)	Halton Road	Confectioners
T.Wright	Halton Road	Butcher & Potato Merchant

1937

Name	Address	Trade/Occupation
F.R.Adams	Church Street	Chemist
B.Appleby	Market Place	Fried Fish Dealer
Geo.Ashton	Simpson Street	Chimney Sweep
J.W.Atkinson	Queen Street	Boot and Shoe Repairer
W.S.Axup	Town Hall	Boot Repairer
Badley & Sons	The Terrace	Motor Car Garage
G.Badley	Cornhill	Hairdresser
Baker & Webb	Ashby Road	Builders
B.E.Balderston	Town Hall	Auctioneer
J.H.Barratt & Son	Boston Road	Coal Merchant
Geo.Bett	Halton Road	Jobbing Gardener
A.Blackburn	'Bull Hotel', Halton Road	Publican
Boston Billposting (E. Beaver)	Halton Road	
Boston Coal Co.	Railway Station, Boston Road	Coal Merchant
C.Buff	Halton Road	Insurance Agent
E.Bull (Mrs.)	Halton Road	Tobacconist
S.Bull	Halton Road	Picture Framer
T.Bundock	Market Place	Photographer
H.Cade	Halton Road	Butcher
R.W.Carr	Market Place and Halton Road	Butcher
J.Cartwright	Market Place	Greengrocer
J.H.Clark	Queen Street	Baker

Name	Address	Trade/Occupation
J.W.Clark	Market Place	Baker
H.A.& E.B.Cooke	Halton Road	Drapers
W.Cossey	Reynard Street	Fried Fish Dealer
J.H.Coulson	Cornhill	Clothier
A.J.Curtis	Market Street	Saddler
H.Davison	Market Street	Ladies' Outfitter
A.E.Dennett	High Street and Queen Street	Dairyman and Grocer
D.Dodds (Mrs.)	Church Street	Apartments
L.S.Dodds	Market Street	Motor Engineers
J.H.Driffield	High Street	Pharmacist
H.Dyas	Queen Street	Newsagent
J.B.Ellerby	Ashby Road	Cowkeeper
R.Ellerby	Newtown	Shopkeeper
W.M.Emerson	'George Hotel', Boston Road,	Publican
E.Ephgrave (Mrs.)	High Street	Confectioner
N.Epton	Halton Road	Shopkeeper
A.C.Farmer (Exors.)	High Street	Chemists
P.Ford	Market Place	Commission Agent
C.J.Fox & Co.	The Terrace	Draper
Franklin Cinema		
F.Garner	High Street	Jeweller
Godsmarks	The Terrace	Drapers and Dressmakers
C.A.Goodrick	High Street	Glass and China Dealers
H.S.Goodrick	Market Street	Butcher
W.F.Goodrick & Sons	Reynard Street and High Street	Joiners & House Furnishers
S.Hanson	Ashby Road	Baker
G.H.Harby	'The Shades', Hundleby Road	Publican
W.T.Harris	Queen Street	Tinsmith
H.Harrison (Mrs.)	High Street	Greengrocer
E.Haw & Sons	Boston Road	Timber Merchants
C.M.Hay	Boston Road	Masseuse
Higgs Bros.	Cornhill	Tobacconists
S.Hilton & Sons Ltd.	The Terrace	Boot Makers
Hunters Stores	Market Street	Grocers
M.B.Jackson & Co.	High Street	Dyers and Cleaners
A.G.Jackson	Ashby Road	Blacksmith
Jeannette	Church Street	Ladies' Outfitters
J.King	Market Place	Grocer
W.J.Kirk	The Terrace	Fishmonger
H.Lake (Mrs.)	High Street	Baker
G.Laming & Sons	Ashby Road	Cabinet Makers
M.I.Laming	Boston Road	Shopkeeper
H.Larder	Market Street	Butcher
J.Lea	Ashby Road	Cow Keeper
E.Lee (Miss.)	High Street	Ladies' Outfitter
Geo.Lenton	High Street	Butcher
Jn.MacDonald	Church Street	Vet
Mackinder, Bennett & Balderston	Town Hall	Auctioneers
G.A.Maddison	Halton Road	Boot Maker

Name	Address	Trade/Occupation
Leo H.Marriott	Ashby Road	Journalist
E.Marshall & Co.	Ashby Road	Wine and Spirit Merchants
H.T.Martin	Boston Road	Registrar of Marriages
H.H.Mawer	Boston Road	Poultry Farmer
E.Miller (Mrs.)	Church Street	Shoe Dealer
L.Moden	Market Street	Café
W.K.Morton & Sons	High Street	Printers
H.C.Moulder	Cornhill	Dentist
Newark Egg Packers	Ashby Road	Egg Merchants
E.Parish (Mrs.)	High Street	Children's Outfitter
J.Parker (Miss.)	High Street	Hairdresser
A.Parratt	The Terrace	Hairdresser
Parsons Bros. & Snape	Boston Road	Coal Merchants
J.Parsons	Ashby Road	Dairyman
R.J.Pinchbeck	Queen Street	Toy Dealer
T.W.Smith	'Queen's Head', Boston Road	Publican
F.G.Rattenbury	Halton Road	Poultry Farmer
A.Richardson	Halton Road	Insurance Agent
F.W.Rimington & Son	Ashby Road	Plumbers etc.
A.J.Rippin	The Terrace	Wireless Dealer
A.W.Rippin	The Terrace	Watchmaker
C.E.Roberts	Boston Road	Motor Engineer
F.Robinson	Boston Road	Builder
H.E.Rogers	'King's Head', Boston Road	Publican
H.Rose	High Street	Tailor and Outfitter
A.Saul	Eresby House	Farmer
A.J.Searby	High Street	Grocer
A.E.Sharp	'Nelson Butt', Market Street	Publican
W.Shaw	Boston Road	Butcher
Shell Mex & BP	Boston Road	
T.W.Simmons	Queen Street	Coal Merchant
Simons, Ingamells & Young	Market Place	Auctioneers & Loss Assessors
W.Sinclair & Sons	Boston Road	Seed Merchants
H.R.Small	High Street	Gents' Outfitter
J.W.Small	Market Place	Builder
Smiths' Fruit Stores	Queen Street	Fruiterers
E.P.Smith	High Street	Dentist
M.Smith (Mrs.)	High Street	Dressmaker
E.Sorfleet (Mrs.)	'Red Lion', Market Place	Publican
F.Sorfleet	Reynard Street	Carriage Builder
W.Sorfleet	Church Street	Confectioners
B.Spence	Halton Road	Grocer
J.E.K.Spence	Queen Street	Tailor
Stead and Simpson	High Street	Boot & Shoe Maker
Stennett, Son & Stevenson	'Shades Hotel' Yard	Auctioneers
Stevenson, Jessap & Co.	The Terrace	Accountants
A.Sylvester	Market Street	Gramophone Dealers
B.Sylvester (Mrs.)	Halton Road	Confectioner
J.M.C.Sylvester	Market Street	Jeweller

APPENDIX I

Occupations of Spilsby inhabitants 1851

Farmers	9 (ex. T.Marshall)
Farm Workers	21
Tradesmen (inc. apprentices & assistants)	92
Craftsmen (inc. apprentices & assistants)	217
Professional people	41
Clerical & services	47
Domestic servants (inc. grooms & ostlers)	185
People of independent means	14
Victuallers	14 (inc. T. Marshall)
Labourers (other than agricultural)	36
Housewives	186
Retired people	14
Paupers	25
Children under 15 (not employed) & all scholars	356
No occupation given	79
Visitors	28
Total	1364
Inhabitants of Spilsby Allotments	44
Prisoners	58
Persons not occupying a house	1
	1467

Occupations in Spilsby in 1851

	Male	Female	Total	Remarks
Domestic Servant	11	150	161	
Shoemaker	61	1	62	includes 29 cordwainers
Labourer (unspecified)	30	1	31	
Tailor	30	1	31	includes "tailors & drapers"
Dressmaker	-	22	22	
Bricklayer	15	-	15	
Groom/Ostler	13	-	13	
Landed Proprietor	5	8	13	
Miller & Baker	12	-	12	
Farmer	10	2	12	
Grocer	9	2	11	
Agricultural labourer	11	-	11	
School teacher	5	5	10	
Ironmonger	10	-	10	
Plumber & Glazier	9	-	9	
Butcher	9	-	9	
Carpenter	8	-	8	
Chairturner	8	-	8	
Saddler	7	-	7	
Blacksmith	7	-	7	
Innkeeper	6	1	7	excludes T. Marshall of the 'White Hart'; he is listed as a farmer.
Solicitor	7	-	7	
Milliner	-	7	7	
Draper	7	-	7	includes "drapers & grocers"
Charwoman	-	6	6	
Clergyman	6	-	6	
Joiner	5	-	5	
Dealer	5	-	5	
Nurse	-	5	5	
Bricklayer's labourer	5	-	5	
Stonemason	4	-	4	
Solicitor's clerk	4	-	4	
Printer	4	-	4	
Doctor	4	-	4	
Brewer	4	-	4	
Laundress	-	4	4	
Errand Boy	4	-	4	
Straw bonnet maker	-	4	4	
Chemist	4	-	4	
Watchmaker	4	-	4	
Hairdresser	3	-	3	
Cabinet maker	3	-	3	
Turnkey	1	2	3	
Carrier	3	-	3	
Veterinary Surgeon	3	-	3	
Postbag	3	-	3	
Builder	3	-	3	
Gardener	3	-	3	
Chandler	3	-	3	
Confectioner	1	2	3	
Hawker	3	-	3	
Ropers	3	-	3	

Male occupations also included:-

Two Curriers, Wheelwrights, Maltsters, Accountants, Whitesmiths, Painters, Higglers, Basket makers, Tinplate workers, Coopers and Yardboys
and ONE Tanner, Surveyor, Banker, Bank Clerk, Bank Agent, Dish-turner, Waggoner, Nailmaker, Sawyer, Brazier, Letter Carrier, Cowkeeper, Horse breaker, Huntsman, Horse clipper, Bellhanger, Clerk, Thatcher, Ironfounder, Hudge Cutter, Haberdasher, Corn-dealer, Drover, Wine & Spirit Merchant, Land Agent, Musician, Organist, Furrier, Silk Merchant, Fishmonger, Soapmaker, Auctioneer, Inland Revenue Officer and Governor of House of Correction.

Female occupations also included:-

Two Cooks
and ONE Wine & Spirit Merchant, Bookseller, Hosier, Furniture Broker, Staymaker, Barmaid, Governess, Needlewoman, Plain Sewing Woman, Haymaker, Beerhouse Keeper and Matron of House of Correction.

Totals:-

Male occupied population   =   434

Female occupied population =   237
                                 ———
                  Total   671
                                 ———

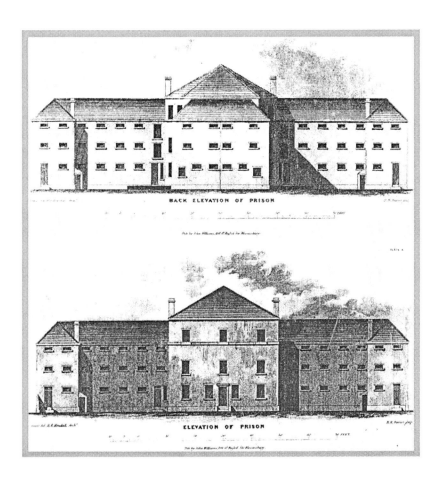

BACK ELEVATION OF PRISON

ELEVATION OF PRISON

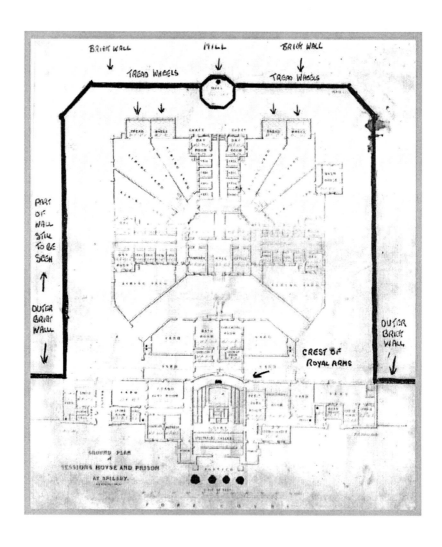

BRICK WALL   MILL   BRICK WALL

TREAD WHEELS   TREAD WHEELS

PART OF WALL STILL TO BE SEEN

OUTER BRICK WALL

OUTER BRICK WALL

CREST OF ROYAL ARMS

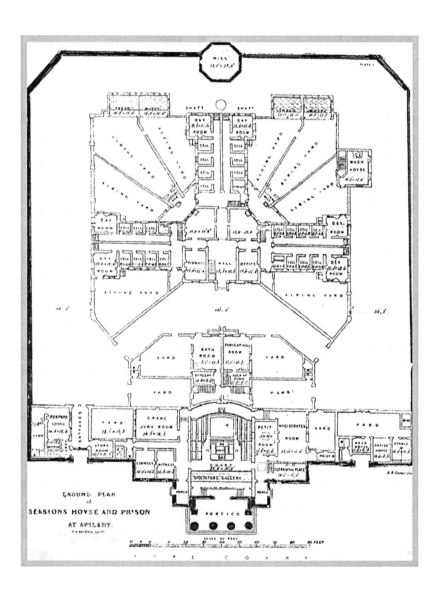

GROUND PLAN
of
SESSIONS HOVSE AND PRISON
AT SPILSBY.

SCALE OF FEET

❖ *Spilsby Radio* ❖

❖ In 1947 Spilsby went "On Air" for the first time when a new wireless amateur transmitting station built by Mr. N.T. Hodgson came into operation. His call sign was G2ABK. His first contact was with another amateur operating from Austria with the call sign OE2XN.

❖ For the first year he was only licensed to use Morse Code but at the end of that time he hoped to be able to install a phone apparatus so he could converse with his contacts.

❖ "Lincolnshire Hamfest" used to meet at the George Hotel in Spilsby. On 27th March radio amateurs from Grimsby, Lincoln, Leicester, Boston and Skegness gathered at a "Junk Sale" at the Bull Hotel in Spilsby.

❖ Spilsby "Hamfest" 26th September 1948.

❖ Spilsby "Hamfest" 1st May 1949.

❖ Spilsby "Hamfest" November 1952.

❖ *The Royal* ❖
British Legion

❖ The following photos are from a British Legion Tea Party at Old Bolingbroke in 1966. This photo shows Dr. Wright patron of the Spilsby Branch fixing the gold badge on Ernie. Looking on is Dick Badley and Frank Surfleet.

❖ This photo shows a group of the members and their families.

❖ This photo dated mid 1960s was taken at British Legion Garden Party at Gunby Hall.

❖ In 1972/3 Spilsby and District British Legion held their Tea Party in the New Town Hall in Spilsby and were entertained by the Stanwell School of Dance.

East Kirkby Airfield

❖ Dedication of the memorial to the members of 57 and 630 Squadrons, who gave their lives in 1939-1945.

Kevin Mapley
(Secretary 207 Squadron Association)

Alec JC White. AG 207 Sqdn 43-44

Kenneth Arm Jeh

Fred Pearce FLT MECH 'F' FREDDY 207

John Pearl Air Gunner 207 SQD.

Michael Madigan, Navigator, 207 Squadron.

❖ This memorial is situated just outside Great Steeping on the old airfield. It is dedicated to all those that lost their lives during the war. 207 Squadron of R.A.F. Spilsby was stationed there.

❖ This photo is of 44 (Rhodesia) Squadron taken at Spilsby Airfield during the war.

End Of An Era

❖ War has broken out and the Spilsby Company are on their way to join the 5th Battalion of the Lincolnshire Territorials [October 1914].

❖ A British Legion Remembrance Parade dated early
1950s [approx].

❖ This photo shows the people of Spilsby on parade to celebrate the coronation of George V in 1910.

❖ *The following photos are of Remembrance Day Parades in the town.*

❖ *This photo was taken at Duxford War Museum in August 2003. I went with the Spilsby Branch of the Royal British Legion. Notice the name on the side of the plane.*

❖ The Spilsby British Legion trip in 2004 was to Fort Paul. These photos were taken there. This photo is of the land army girls having a rest after a hard day's work.

❖ This photo shows me trying out the sidecar seat of a
World War II motorbike.

❖ The British Legion trip on the 24ᵗʰ June 2006 was to
Eden Camp in North Yorkshire.
❖ Me on guard duty.

❖ *My Dad having a rest.*

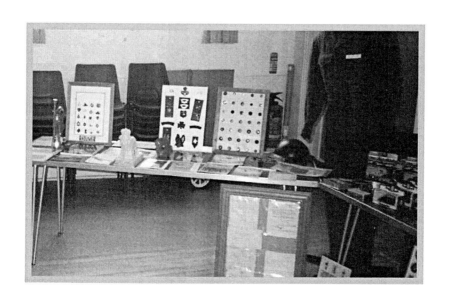

❖ This photo is from a show that my Dad did for the Legion at Spilsby Town Hall in September 2004. It was organised by the Spilsby and District History Society.

❖ These two photos were taken at the Poppy Appeal Launch at East Kirkby in October 2004.

BRITISH LEGION 105742

....Branch.

....19

RECEIVED of...

the sum of ....s.......d. in respect of Membership

Subscription for 1 YEAR ending...............................19

....Branch Secretary.

IMPORTANT.

If you change your address please inform your Branch Secretary.

❖ These two documents show copies of a membership card
and receipt from 1945.

Name of Branch *SPILSBY & DISTRICT*

Member's Name *MR R. BARKER*

Address *MASONIC LANE.*

HUNDLEBY, SPILSBY

Badge No. — Date of joining *11. 10. 46*

ENTRANCE FEE, ONE SHILLING, PAID.

Signature
of Member } * _____

PRINCIPLES AND POLICY OF THE BRITISH LEGION.

(a). The Legion shall be democratic, non-sectarian, and shall not be affiliated to or connected directly or indirectly with any political party or political organisation.

(b). The Legion shall be created to inaugurate and maintain in a strong, stimulating, united and democratic comradeship, all those who have served in His Majesty's Navy, Army, Air Force, or any Auxiliary Forces, so that neither their efforts nor their interests shall be forgotten; that their welfare and that of the dependants of the fallen may be safeguarded; and that just and equitable treatment shall be secured to them in respect of the difficulties caused in their lives as a result of their services.

(c). The Legion shall exist to perpetuate in the civil life of the Empire and of the World the principles for which we have fought; to inculcate a sense of loyalty to the Crown, Community, State, and Nation; to promote unity amongst all classes; to make right the master of might; to secure peace and goodwill on earth; to safeguard and transmit to posterity the principles of justice, freedom, and democracy, and to consecrate and sanctify our comradeship by our devotion to mutual service and helpfulness.

The attention of the holder of this card is specially drawn to the following extracts from Rule 2.

(e). Any person accepted as an Ordinary Member shall be deemed to be a Member so long as his name remains upon the Membership Register provided that the said Member has not resigned or died and that his membership has not otherwise lapsed or been determined for good and sufficient reasons by the decision of the Branch to which he belongs. Any Member whose arrears of contributions do not exceed the amount represented by three months contribution shall be deemed to be a financial Member and as such shall be entitled to vote and otherwise take part in the affairs of the Legion.

(g). Any Ordinary Member who is three months in arrears in respect of his contributions under Rule 2 (z) shall be liable to have his Membership determined by the decision of the Branch of which he is a Member.

(h). No Ordinary Member holding an official position of any description in the Legion shall be in arrears with contributions under Rule 2 (z) except upon pain of forfeiture of the position held by him.

(i). Any Ordinary Member producing satisfactory evidence to his Branch that he is unable through unemployment or ill-health to maintain his contributions may be permitted to remain a full Member notwithstanding non-payment of such contributions for such period and upon such terms as the Branch Committee may determine.

Copyright.

❖ These letters were sent to Legion Members requesting them to attend the funerals of two of their members. One was their late President and the other their late Secretary.

Spilsby & District Branch.

Sir,

You are requested to attend the Funeral of our late President, Colonel G. B. Walker, V.D., on FRIDAY, 8th OCTOBER, 1926.

Members will assemble at the Roman Catholic Church at 10.45 a.m.

Yours sincerely,

JOHN M. MORTON,
Hon. Sec.

In Respectful Remembrance of
Col. G. B. WALKER, V.D.,
who departed this life 4th October, 1926,
Aged 64 years.

BRITISH LEGION

(SPILSBY BRANCH.)

FRANKLIN HOUSE,

SPILSBY.

Sir,

The Funeral of our late Secretary, Mr. John M. Morton, will take place at Spilsby, on Wednesday, 26th October, 1927, at 2 p.m.

The Chairman hopes that as many members as possible will attend, and assemble in Spence Street, Spilsby (near the Church) at 1.45 p.m.

Medals will be worn.

Yours faithfully,

F. LAMING,
Hon. Sec. *(pro. tem.)*

❖ The following photos were taken at the Spilsby Show on Sunday 9th July 2006. It shows members of the Legion putting on their displays.

❖ *Collection owned by Mr. D. Odlin.*

❖ *Mr. R. Worth*

❖ *Driver Mr. T. Humphries.*

Arthur Benjamin

❖ Tayles ❖

❖ *Arthur was born in Walmsgate, Louth in 1918. Arthur married Edna at Spilsby Church on November 4th 1936.*

❖ They lived in Franklin Passage until 1942, then moved to Reynard Street where he ran his own fruit and veg shop until 1977 (approx). During his life Arthur worked for L. Dodds as a store keeper, he was also an ambulance driver from 1958-1968 then part-time from 1978-1983.

❖ Arthur joined the 4ᵗʰ Royal Lincolnshire Regiment and fought during World War II. He was stationed in Iceland, involved in the raids on Norway and Nijmegan Bridge. Arthur's Regiment had also been involved with the capture of Arnhem.

❖ Arthur's brother W.H. Tayles who was also in the 4th Lincolnshire Regiment was killed on the 8th March 1943 aged 22 years.

❖ *Four other local men served in the same Regiment with Arthur, they were brothers Colin and Allan Wilkinson, Colin Hartley and Major Jessop.*

❖ For 63 years Arthur kept an allotment down Post Office Lane in Spilsby. He was also Chairman and President of Spilsby Town Football Club for many years. Arthur was also a member of the Spilsby Branch of the Royal British Legion and also the Buffs. Whilst on holiday in 1988 Arthur visited his brother's grave. Arthur died 17th July 2002.

❖ *School Life* ❖

❖Spilsby Grammar School around the 1900s. Note the cannon sat outside the school.

❖ The school was a boys only school when it first opened. In 1911 it had 27 boys on the register but by 1914 girls were accepted into the grammar school.

❖ Also around 1914 a small private school was opened in Church Street, it was for pupils whose parents were better off and could pay for their children's education.

❖ School life has changed a lot over the years. The three pictures below date from the early 1900s to the mid 1900s. The school was called the Spilsby National School and was on Halton Road. The children in the photos were aged from 7-11 years of age.

❖ In the early 1900s the school claimed to have room for 250 children but only had about 150 attending. In 1905 the school was run by only 2 full-time qualified teachers.

❖ The school closed its doors in the late 1980s. The children would attend a new junior school, which was built on to the infant school in Woodlands Avenue. The building site was once part of the Franklin Schools field.

y in the hall of the new school, where sub-constructing cupboards and fittings on the remises. (Photo: Ben Hardaker).

Workmen positioning slabs outside the new school. (Photo: Ben Hardaker).

ilders on target for school opening

THE new building for the juniors at Spilsby Primary School is well in line for completion in time for the official opening by the Canadian High Commissioner on April 16 — the bi-centenary of the birth of explorer Sir John Franklin.

The new part of the school, which has been built on to the existing infants' school — in what was part of the Franklin School playing fields — should be completed by its scheduled date of March 31. The only possible problem is the completion of what remains of the outside work, which is being held up by the weather.

The headmaster, Mr Eric Damms, says the new school building's most dramatic effect will be to cut out the commuting between the old school and the infants' school, which are something like half a mile apart.

"There was no unity between the two," he said. "The infants never felt part of the primary school.

"Another real bonus will be having a school hall, with the space element and the PE equipment. We have never had a school hall before, and had to crowd into a classroom for morning assembly," he pointed out.

The new school will be a great improvement on the early Victorian one in Halton Road. All the classrooms will be carpeted, and plans are afoot to bring the infants' section into line with it later in the year. Gas central heating has been installed.

The new school will be virtually full from the outset. It is designed, together with the infants' section, to hold 180 pupils. The present school roll is 177, with more to come after Easter.

❖ *This is a copy of the plan for the new school extension also a newspaper article on how the work was getting on.*

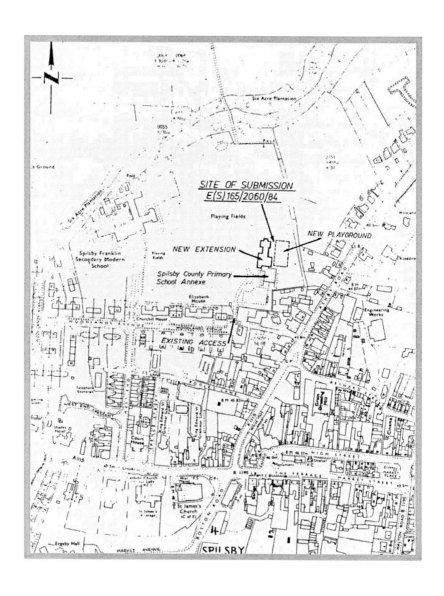

SITE OF SUBMISSION
E(S)165/2060/84

NEW PLAYGROUND

NEW EXTENSION

Spilsby County Primary
School Annexe

EXISTING ACCESS

Spilsby Franklin
Secondary Modern
School

SPILSBY

❖ *Hospitals* ❖

The Poor House

❖ Spilsby Union Workhouse was built in 1837. It was situated at the south side of Hundleby Road and to the west of Spilsby.

❖ It was intended to house 260 inmates and it cost around £3,500.

❖ The architects were partners George Gilbert Scott and William Bonython Moffat, who were also responsible for designing the workhouses in Boston, Louth and Horncastle.

❖ The menu for the poor that lived there consisted of
Breakfast - Milk or Broth
Dinner - Dumplings, Cold Meat, or Sheep Heads.
Supper - Bread and Cheese, Milk or Dumplings

❖ When it was opened it had
1. Eight children under 12 years.
2. One man, one woman over 70 years old.
3. One woman aged 35 years.
4. Fourteen pensioners.

❖ The people had to get up at 6.00a.m. and go to bed at
9.00p.m. The doors were locked at 8.30p.m. every night.

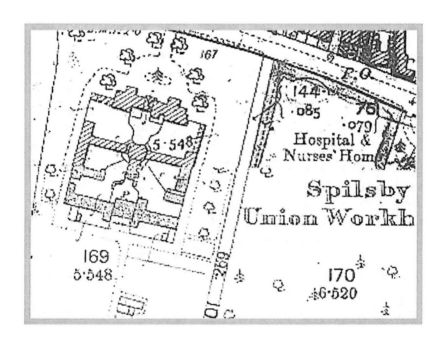

❖ *The map shows the layout of the workhouse in 1904.*

❖ *This photo shows the main block from the North-East in 2001.*

❖ The Grace Swan Memorial Hospital in the 1920s. When the hospital was first opened in May 1920, it only had four beds but seven years later an operating theatre was added.

❖ The hospital closed a few years ago and is now a health centre. Several private houses have been built in the old car park.

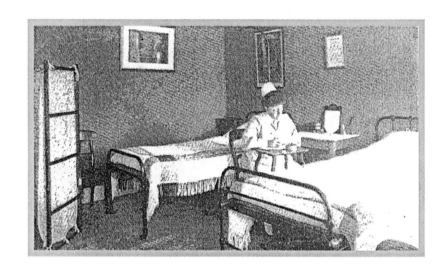

❖ *A nurse writing up patients notes at the hospital.*

❖ Churches ❖

❖ The Roman Catholic Church of our Lady and the English Martyrs.

❖ This photo shows St. James Parish Church around 1846.

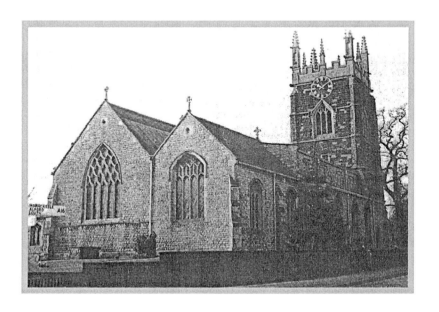

❖ In the early 1870s an inn called The White Horse was demolished and on the site a Wesleyan church was built. It had a pair of manses for the ministers and was opened in 1878. Before this they used to worship in a square brick chapel, which was erected at the beginning of the century in Wellington Yard.

❖ This photo shows Spilsby Methodist Sunday School in front of the chapel around 1926 (approx).

❖ *This transcript is of the Register of Baptisms, Marriages and Burials in Spilsby during 1743-4*

Spilsby 1743

March 29 Elizabeth Gregory Wid: buried.
John Son of John and Anne Hunstone buried.
April Frances Wife of Mr Nathaniel Graby buried.
Robert Son of Robert and Faith Ward bapt:
28 Thomas Smith and Susanna Smith married.
May Anne Daug: of John and Mary Buxe bapt:
19 Mary Smith Wid: buried.
21 Thomas Brough buried.
27 Anne Daug: of William and Anne Gregory bapt:
28 Elizabeth Burgess (a stranger) buried.
31 Anne Daug: of Rich: Gill buried.
June 1 Charles Son of Francis and Anne Humpstone bapt:
2 John Son of Thomas and Frances Bright coll: bapt:
4 John Son of Joshua and Robecca Barker bapt:
7 Anne Daug of Thomas and Elizabeth Baslington bapt:
9 Susanna Daug: of William Shepherd Jun: and Elizabeth his Wife
28 John Bocroft and Mary Key married.
July 15 Mary Daug: of William and Elizabeth Parker bapt:
17 Samuel Son of William and Rose Barnet bapt:
Joseph Son of Francis and Elizabeth Sims (strangers) bapt:
29 Hannah Wife of Thomas Birch buried.
Aug: 20 Eliza-Catharina Wife of Mr William Brackenbury burit:
Elizabeth Wife of Mr George Wright buried.
21 George Son of George Blew of Faithby buried.
22 Sarah Daug of William and Sarah Leland bapt:
29 The said Sarah buried
Sep: 12 Robert Son of Robert Hastings Gent and Anna Maria his Wife bapt:
Oct 20 Anne Graby buried.
26 William Richison and Rachel Maw married.
31 Susanna Daug: of John and Mary Jackson bapt:
Nov 2 The said Susanna buried
10 John Son of Mr John Laine and Susanna his Wife bapt:
23 Edna Daug: of John and Rebecca Gunnis bapt:
24 Edward Son of George and Mary Smith buried.
30 William Son of Joseph and Elizabeth Wright bapt:
Dec 16 Joseph Acred & Martha Brough married.
21 Robert Wright buried.
23 Mary Daug: of John and Jane Acred bapt:
26 John Anderton buried.
Jan: 4 William Son of William and Mary Clark bapt:
18 William Son of Joseph and Elizabeth Wright buried.
24 Mary Daug: of Edward and Anne Gunby bapt:
March the 25th 1744.

195

❖ *Eresby House* ❖

❖ The town of Spilsby was mostly the property of Lord Willoughby de Eresby. Eresby was a tiny hamlet half a mile to the south and had 11 inhabitants.

❖ Eresby House was built in the 1530s and was destroyed by fire in 1769. The house was built by Charles Brandon, Duke of Suffolk shortly after his marriage to Lady Catherine Willoughby, daughter of the last Lord Willoughby de Eresby. The house was built in a H shape.

❖ After the fire all that remained was one gate pillar. No painting or sketch of the home survived the fire.

THE AVENUE, S█████

❖   *If you stood outside* The Shades Hotel, *you could look straight down the tree-lined* Avenue *and see the grand house, as the picture below shows.*

❖ *This drawing is of the Pillars of Eresby, as they would have looked around 1791. The Pillars were to be made into one soon after this sketch was done.*

❖ Ice skating on Eresby pond during winter, 1920s.

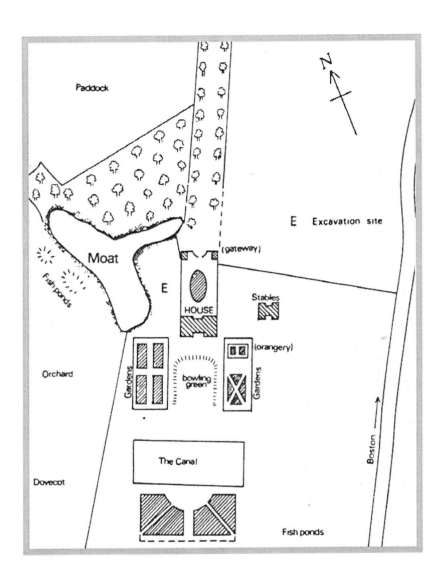

Labels within the image:
Paddock
N
E Excavation site
Moat
(gateway)
E
Fish ponds
HOUSE
Stables
(orangery)
Orchard
Gardens
bowling green
Gardens
Boston
The Canal
Dovecot
Fish ponds

❖ *This is a plan of Eresby House, as it would have been when it was first built.*

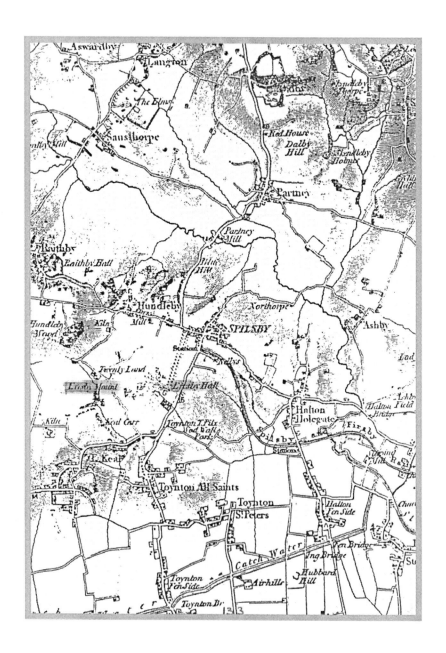

❖ Celebrations ❖

❖ The following three photos were taken during the celebration of the coronation of King George V and Queen Mary in 1910.

❖ This photo shows Maypole dancing in the Avenue,
Sunday School children and Boy Scouts took part.

❖ This photo shows the Spilsby Rechabites, Volunteers and Fire Brigade [with hand pump] in the middle market place.

❖ This photo shows the celebrations continuing in the middle market place with more Maypole dancing.

❖ *The following photos show some of the celebrations that I have enjoyed during my life so far.*

❖ *Remembrance parade 2002.*

❖ Launch of the poppy appeal 2002, which was opened by
Sir Richard Todd.

THE QUEEN'S GOLDEN JUBILEE SPILSBY

PRESS RELEASE

At the final meeting of the Spilsby Golden Jubilee Committee on Jan 20th nine year old Kelly Odlin received first prize for the album she entered for the Jubilee photographic album competition. Kelly, pictured above, received her Golden Jubilee commemorative coin and winner's certificate from committee member Jim Swanson. Her album of pictures contained photographs taken at the June 3rd celebrations in the town centre and included a nice shot of the Spitfire as it over-flew the parade.

Afterwards a statement of accounts was presented by committee chairman Jim Woolley and it was decided that the surplus funds amounting to £1577 would be spent on a community notice board subject to finding an appropriate site in the town centre.

Spilsby Golden Jubilee Committee, Jan 27th 2003

Parish of Spilsby

Celebration of the Coronation of their Majesties
King George VI and Queen Elizabeth

Wednesday, 12th May, 1937

Programme of the
Celebrations

arranged for Spilsby

1 Church Parade of Public Bodies	5 Decorated Vehicles Parade
	6 Teas for Children and for Adults
2 Presentation of Seats for use of Public	7 Beakers for Children
3 Competition for Decoration of Buildings	8 Athletic Sports for all
	9 Whist Drive
4 Children's Fancy Dress Parade	10 Carnival Dance

The competitions are open to Spilsby Residents only.

● ADMISSION TO THE TEAS WILL BE BY TICKET ONLY ●

Programme.

9.30 a.m.   Members of all Public Bodies will assemble on the Butter Market for Church Parade, headed by the Spilsby Town Band.

10 a.m.   Joint Service at the Spilsby Parish Church.

10.45 a.m.   Spilsby Cross Roads. Presentation of two Seats for use of public by Spilsby Gala Committee to Spilsby Parish Council.

This ceremony will be brief, to allow those who wish to return home to listen to the broadcast of the actual Coronation Ceremony.

1 p.m.   **Decorated Premises Competition.**

Judging will be commenced.

Areas and prizes are:

Class A. Shops, Offices, Hotels. 3 prizes: £2, £1, 10/-.
Inside window dressing will be ignored.

Class B. Group 1. Halton Road
     2. Simpson Street
     3. Alma Place
     4. New Town
     5. Queen St., Wellington Gardens and Post Office Lane
     6. Reynard Street and Franklin Square
     7. Boston Road, Vale and Farm Cottages
     8. Ashby Road and Poole's Lane
     9. Church Street, Spence Street and West End
     10. Partney Road and Hundleby Road
     11. Masonic Lane
     12. Lower Market Place, High Street, Cornhill and Terrace (excluding all shops)

Twelve Groups. First prize of 10/-, Second prize of 5/- to each Group.

Prizes will be awarded according to the possibilities of the premises and the means of the residents, thus every house and shop will have an equal chance of success.

It is *not* necessary to enter. Every house and shop will be inspected.

2.30 p.m.

Children's Fancy Dress Competition
Decorated Vehicles Competition

(All entrants assemble at 2.15 p.m. at School, Halton Road).

It is *not* necessary to enter names previously. Classes and awards will be :

Children's Fancy Dress	Prizes 1st	2nd	3rd	4th
1. Children under 8 years, Girls,	valued 10/-	6/-	3/-	1/6
Boys,	valued 10/-	6/-	3/-	1/6
2. Children under 12 years, Girls,	10/-	6/-	3/-	1/6
Boys,	10/-	6/-	3/-	1/6
3. Children under 16 years, Girls,	valued 12/6	6/- val'd 3/-		1/6
Boys,	valued 12/6	6/-	3/-	1/6
4. Adults, original comic or partners	20/-	10/-	5/-	—
5. Decorated Perams. & Pushchairs	val'd 10/-	val'd 7/6	val'd 5/-	—
6. Decorated Cycles & Motor Cycles	val'd 15/-	val'd 10/-	val'd 5/-	—
7. Decorated Private Cars	20/-	15/-	5/-	—
8. Decorated Trade Vans	20/-	15/-	10/-	—

Vouchers will be given except where prize is an article. These vouchers *must* be cashed at a Spilsby shop within one week.

4 p.m.

Children's Tea in the Drill Hall

Admission of children and their mothers will be by ticket only. Mothers wishing to be with their children will be welcomed at the Drill Hall. Tickets obtainable from Mr. Taylor, St. James' School, on request by scholars also from Mackinder, Bennett & Balderston's office, 2.30 to 5 p.m., Saturday, 1st May, and 7 to 9 p.m., Wednesday, 5th May, to allow efficient catering, no tickets will be issued after Wednesday, 5th May.

4 p.m.

Meat Tea for Adults in Wesleyan Schoolroom

All residents over 16th birthday attend at Wesleyan Schoolroom; under 16 at Drill Hall. Admission by ticket only, to allow efficient catering. Tickets obtainable from Mackinder, Bennett & Balderston's office at above-stated times, also from Dadleys' shop and the Cinema at any time. No tickets will be issued after Wednesday, 5th May. Every adult *must* bring own knife, fork and spoon.

4 to 5 p m.

Beakers for Children

These will have handles and will be used for tea. Beakers are available for every child of all ages below 17th birthday. Children taking tea will be given their beakers. Parents of other children must collect these beakers at the entrance to the Drill Hall, 4 to 5 p.m. No beakers will be delivered, nor can they be collected at any other time or place.

5.30 to 7.30 p.m. **Athletic Sports for all, on Grammar School Field, Partney Road**

It is *not* necessary to register names previously to entering the field. The Town Band will play on the field.

Events and prizes are:

1.	60 yds. Flat, Boys under 9	1/6	1/-	6d.
2.	60 " Girls "	1/6	1/-	6d.
3.	90 " Boys " 13	3/-	2/-	1/-
4.	100 " Men, open	20/-	10/-	5/-
5.	3-legged, Girls under 11	2/-	1/-	—
6.	Cigarette Race, Mixed Pairs, open	5/-	3/-	2/-
7.	100 yds. Flat, Boys under 17	7/6	5/-	2/-
8.	90 " Girls " 13	3/-	2/-	1/-
9.	75 " Men, Veterans over 60	10/-	5/-	2/6
10.	220 " Men, open	10/-	5/-	2/6
11.	Obstacle Race, Mixed, under 11	3/-	2/-	1/-
12.	100 yds. Flat, Women, open	10/-	5/-	2/6
13.	Egg and Spoon, Girls under 11	1/-	6d.	—
14.	1 mile Flat, Men, open	20/-	10/-	5/-
15.	Obstacle Race, Mixed, over 11	5/-	3/-	2/-
16.	Egg and Spoon, Women, open	5/-	3/-	2/-
17.	100 yds. Flat, Girls under 17	7/6	5/-	2/6
18.	Apple Race, Mixed, open	7/6	5/-	2/6

8 p.m. **Whist Drive (12 hands).**

In the Drill Hall. Admission 6d. including Dance.
Prizes: Ladies 20/-, 10/-, 7/6, 5/-, 2/6, 2/6.
Gents ditto

9 p.m. to 2 a.m. **Carnival Dance.**

Admission 6d. (including Whist Drive).
Participants are invited to wear Fancy Dress upon this happy occasion.

Special Souvenirs.

Souvenirs, suitably inscribed, will be presented to any children born during Coronation week (Sunday, 9th to Saturday, 15th May inclusive) to Parents resident in Spilsby. Claims to Mr. J. N. Radford (Registrar of Births).

Spilsby Coronation Committee.

Chairman: Capt. W. Cowling.

Executive Sub-committee: Mrs. G. M. Dean, Dr. C. S. E. Wright, Mr. A. W. Nesbitt, Mr. C. F. Farmer, Mr. G. Rutter.

Chairmen of Sub-committees:

Catering: Mrs. H. T. Martin
Decorated Premises: Mr. S. Rattenbury
Children's Fancy Dress, etc.: Mr. C. F. Farmer
Athletic Sports: Mr. A. W. Nesbitt
Whist Drive and Dance: Mr. J. N. Radford
Bandmaster: Mr. Geo. Laming
Parade Marshal: Mr. F. Jobson
Dance Band: Mr. A. Backhouse, Wainfleet

Hon. Auditor: Mr. S. A. Farmer

Hon. Secretary & Treasurer: Mr. A. E. Watts

❖ *Sports* ❖

❖ In the early 1900s Spilsby used to have its own Ladies Hockey Club, Spilsby Cricket Club, Football Club, Angling Club and a Lawn Tennis Club. The Cricket Club was formed in 1880 (approx). A lawn tennis club followed in 1884 as part of the cricket club and by 1900 a hockey club, golf club and cycling club had also been formed. In 1913-1914 season Spilsby United was the most successful football team in the district.

The Spilsby Ladies Hockey Club — the 'Eresby Club', 1911.

The Spilsby Cricket Club, 1908.

❖ The all-conquering Spilsby Football Team of 1913-1914.

❖ Top row left to right: W. Maughan, J. Ely, W. Barker, E. Boyall, J. Boyall Rev. G. Rigall, B. Boyall.

❖ Bottom row: M.W. Kirk, G.F. Barker, J.W. Sylvester, G.W. Holderness.

❖ *Spilsby Angling Association at a fishing match at Eresby pond in the 1900s.*

SPILSBY FOOTBALL TEAM
WINNERS OF THE
Lincolnshire Association Challenge Cup
AT
BRIGG

SPILSBY FOOTBALL
—Champions of Lincolnshire

Spilsby Football Team were the first winners of the Lincolnshire Cup in the days before professionalism—in 1881-2—defeating Lincoln Rovers, Gainsborough Trinity and (in the final) Brigg Town. They repeated the performance in the following two seasons (beating Grimsby in the 1883-4 final), and thus won the trophy outright. They were, indeed, the champions of Lincolnshire.

Spilsby's next success did not come until 12 years later when in 1896 the Rovers defeated Brigg in the final of the Lincolnshire Shield. There followed 18 lean years, the old Spilsby Town putting a team in the field with great regularity without achieving much success in competitions. However, they were regarded everywhere as a fine sporting side. The Town F.C. ran into trouble with the Lincolnshire F.A. and was disbanded. For two seasons local football was represented by Spilsby Territorials, whose career ended in the season 1910-11. Before the next season started it was decided to form a new club—Spilsby United.

The soccer season of 1913-14 saw Spilsby football at its zenith. The United with very few exceptions, fielded the same side for most of the season. After an indifferent start the players gradually settled down and within a few months had become one of the best amateur sides in East-Mid-North Lincolnshire. Indeed, after the third week in November 1913 they went right to the end of the season without defeat. Curiously, there was one team Spilsby could not beat that year—old rivals in Skegness United; there were several drawn games in league matches but the Seasiders were not overcome.

In the 1913-14 season the best amateur club in North Lincolnshire was Grimsby Haycroft Rovers, but in the Isthmian Cup the Rovers were defeated by their neighbours, Grimsby St. John. It was the latter team, that met Spilsby United in the final of the Isthmian Cup at Louth. There was tremendous enthusiasm in Spilsby and district on the day of the final. A special train took a big crowd of supporters to Louth and many others made their way by bicycle and wagonette. (No motor buses in those days!)

Spilsby faced their most formidable opponents of that season with the will to win but realised the magnitude of the task. It was a great struggle with both sides attacking with all their might, and it was not until the last few minutes of the game that Spilsby triumped by three goals to two. A fortnight later Spilsby gained a second trophy, defeating Louth Trinity (forerunners of Louth Town) in the final of the Cusworth Cup.

That Spilsby side never played together again, for a few months later World War One broke out on the battlefields of France and Belgium. Practically the whole side was in khaki on the day the war started mobilising with the Spilsby Company of the 5th Lincs Territorials, and by 1915 four members of the team had made the supreme sacrifice.

concluded on page 4

Spilsby United F.C.
1913-14
Winners of Isthmian
and Cusworth Cups

Standing (L to R): W. C. Maughan, J. Ely, W. Barker, E. Boyall, J. Boyall, Revd G. H. Riggall, B. Boyall. Sitting (L to R): W. M. Kirk, G. F. Barker, J. W. Sylvester, G. W. Holdemess.

❖ *The following sheets of paper are the winners from the Spilsby Domino League dating from 1967-2004.*

❖ *Also a list of members gone but not forgotten.*

Spilsby Domino League

Season	Domino Out	5's & 3's	Headquarte
1967-1968	Shades	George	Kings Head
1968-1969	Kings Head 'A'	George	Hundleby
1969-1970	George	Kings Head 'A'	Red Lion
1970-1971	George	George	Partney
1971-1972	George	George	White Hart
1972-1973	George	George	Nelson
1973-1974	George 'A'	George 'B'	Bull
1974-1975	Red Lion 'B'	White Hart	George
1975-1976	Red Lion 'B'	Red Lion 'B'	Red Lion
1976-1977	George	White Hart 'A'	Bull
1977-1978	George	George	Partney
1978-1979	Queen's Head	George	Nelson
1979-1980	Queen's Head	Hundleby 'A'	Red Lion
1980-1981	Hundleby 'B'	George	White Hart
1981-1982	Hundleby 'A'	George	Hundleby
1982-1983	White Hart	White Hart	Queen's Head
1983-1984	White Hart	White Hart	George
1984-1985	White Hart	Hundleby 'C'.	Queen's Head
1985-1986	Nomads	Tongs	White Hart
1986-1987	Hundleby 'A'	Hundleby 'A'	Hundleby
1987-1988	George 'A'	White Hart	George
1988-1989	Tongs	Hundleby 'B'	Nelson
1989-1990	Hundleby 'A'	George 'A'	Shades
1990-1991	White Hart 'A'	Kings Head 'A'	White Hart
1991-1992	George 'A'	Besco	Hundleby
1992-1993	Hundleby 'A'	Shades 'A'	George
1993-1994	George 'A'	Hundleby 'B'	Nelson
1994-1995	George 'A'	George 'A'	Shades
1995-1996	Hundleby	Nomads	Red Lion
1996-1997	Shades	White Hart 'A'	White Hart
1997-1998	Shades 'B'	Shades 'B'	Hundleby
1998-1999	George 'A'	White Hart 'B'	George
1999-2000	White Hart 'A'	George 'B'	Nelson
2000-2001	Nomads	George 'B'	Shades
2001-2002	White Hart	George 'B'	Red Lion
2002-2003	Shades	Shades	White Hart
2003-2004	Shades	Bell	Nelson

Spilsby Domino League

Season	Domino Out Knockout	5's & 3's Knockout
1967-1968	E. Daubner & D. Shucksmith	K. Hough & J. Hancock
1968-1969	W. Hudson & R. Oliver	M. Woods & M. Briggs
1969-1970	K. Hough & J. Hancock	J. Wooley & D. Sawyer
1970-1971	M. Woods & B. Leishman	B. Philpot & F. Redford
1971-1972	P. Hancock & J. Wooley	J. Tarrant & J. Tarrant
1972-1973	A. Barker & G. Matthews	K. Hough & A. Bache
1973-1974	J. Wooley & J. Gunson	A. Barker & G. Matthews
1974-1975	M. Dobbs & M. Howard	R. Wisby & D.Shucksmith
1975-1976	K. Hough & A. Bache	A. Mountain & G. Wydell
1976-1977	K. Hough & A. Bache	E. Waltham & E. Waltham
1977-1978	J. Tarrant & J. Tarrant	R. Chapman & B. Rymer
1978-1979	W. Mutton & H. Ellerby	P. Blanchard & C. Spring

1979-1980	J. Bird & B. Pogson	M. Woods & R. Oliver
1980-1981	I. Bogg & B. Pailing	G. Wydell & J. Emery
1981-1982	G. Tuplin & G. Wood	F. Drinkell & T. Hewitt
1982-1983	D. Mowbray & D. Shucksmith	P. Blanchard & E. Hubbard
1983-1984	R. Hewis & M. Pawson	R. Chapman & J. Wooley
1984-1985	R. Hutchins & B. Hutchins	J. Bird & M. Kettle
1985-1986	M. Holland & H. Leverton	R. Hutchins & B. Hutchins
1986-1987	S. Smith & M. Holland	E. Bryan & B. Chapman
1987-1988	R. Blades & F. Tempest	M. Woods & M. Ford
1988-1989	R. Oliver & P. Middleton	E. Bryan & P. Evison
1989-1990	B. Philpot & G. Pawson	D. Mowbray & H. Ellerby
1990-1991	D. Hewitt & A. Bogg	D. Hewitt & J. Rushby
1991-1992	K. Sylvester & O. Smith	K. Hough & J. Gunson
1992-1993	D. Shucksmith & L. Shucksmith	E. Bryan & P. Evison
1993-1994	M. Holland & H. Leverton	M. Mutton & H. Brown

1994-1995	M. Holland & H. Leverton	K. Hough & J. Gunson
1995-1996	T. Hewitt & R. Hubbard	K. Sylvester & C. Pagram
1996-1997	R. Chapman & M. Holland	K. Sylvester & C. Pagram
1997-1998	K. Hough & T. Hewitt	R. Hubbard & G. Tuplin
1998-1999	D. Odlin & P. Evison	K. Hough & T. Hewitt
1999-2000	R. Shelley & T. Maguire	R. Shelley & T. Maguire
2000-2001	D. Blanchard & A. Tayles	D. Mowbray & G. Davison
2001-2002	M. Woods & M. Ford	D. Mowbray & G. Davison
2002-2003	A. Mountain & R. Nelson	P. Robinson & K. Gunson

Knockout Trophy Winners

Name	Domino Out	5's & 3's	Tony Bach
K. Hough	4	4	1
M. Woods	2	3	1
D. Mowbray	1	3	1
T. Hewitt	2	2	1
J. Woolley	2	2	0
E. Bryan	0	3	1
R. Chapman	1	2	1
D. Shucksmith	3	1	0
P. Evison	1	2	1
A. Bache	2	1	0
R. Oliver	2	1	0
Mi. Holland	3	0	0
H. Leverton	3	0	0
R. Hutchins	1	1	1
B. Hutchins	1	1	1
K. Sylvester	1	2	0
P. Blanchard	0	2	1
G. Tuplin	1	1	1
G. Davison	0	1	1
B. Philpot	1	1	1
J. Gunson	0	2	0
J. Hancock	1	1	0
A. Barker	1	1	0
G. Matthews	1	1	0
J. Tarrant (jnr)	1	1	0
J. Tarrant (snr)	1	1	0
J. Bird	1	1	0
H. Ellerby	1	1	0
D. Hewitt	1	1	1
C. Pagram	0	2	0
R. Hubbard	1	1	0
R. Shelley	1	1	0
T. Maguire	1	1	0
R. Nelson	1	0	2

Tony Bache Memorial Trophy

Year	Winners
1981-1982	K. Hough & C. Bryant
1982-1983	M. Woods & D. Wright
1983-1984	D. Sawyer & W. Short
1984-1985	P. Blanchard & E. Hubbard
1985-1986	P. Gibson & M. Gibson
1986-1987	M. Philpot & B. Philpot
1987-1988	B. Hutchins & R. Hutchins
1988-1989	E. Bond & E. Oliver
1989-1990	R. Chapman & M. Wells
1990-1991	E. Bryan & P. Evison
1991-1992	D. Wright & B. Pailing
1992-1993	D. Mowbray & D. Mackinder
1993-1994	M. Fothergill & D. Fothergill
1994-1995	G. Griffin & L. Haigh
1995-1996	G. Davison & R. Nelson
1996-1997	M. Mutton & J. Payne
1997-1998	N. Odlin & R. Cornall
1998-1999	D. Mackinder & J.Lee
1998-2000	T. Hewit & G. Tuplin
2000-2001	A. Mountain & R. Nelson
2001-2002	H. Lillie & I. Brough
2002-2003	C. Tempest & D. Hewitt

Members Gone But Not Forgotten

R. Brough	D. Brough	E. Bond
A. Bond	A. Bache	W. Bache
G. Barber	A. Barker	T. Barker
J. Beardsley	F. Bland	H. Bogg
H. Brown	K. Burgess	T. Bird
P. Blanchard	J. Cabon	B. Chapman
T. Clark	R. Clifton	J. Dickinson
J. Ellis	H. Ellerby	A. Fothergill
R. Garrard	R. Hewis	E. Holderness
S. Holderness	K. Hough	W. Hudson
P. Hancock	J. Hancock	E. Hubbard
R. Hubbard	T. Hewitt	S. King
P. Lowis	H. Mutton	G. Matthews
R. Oliver	G. Oliver	M. Protas
F. Redford	P. Starmer	R. Spence
S. Storr	G. Tuplin	J. Tarrant
F. Tempest	A. Tayles	W. Towle
W. Wallis	E. Waltham	G. Wydell

REST IN PEACE

❖ Family Tree ❖

Modified Register for Joseph Odlin

First Generation

1 Joseph Odlin was born about 1724. He died in May 1803 and was buried[1] on 24 May 1803 in Tetford, Lincolnshire.

Joseph was employed as Baker.

Joseph married[2] **Mary Thomlinson** on 14 Sep 1754 in Tetford, Lincolnshire. Mary was born about 1732. She died in 1799 and was buried[3] on 15 Jul 1799 in Tetford, Lincolnshire.

They had the following children:

     2 M   i. **Joseph Odlin** was born about 1761 and was buried on 21 Apr 1794.

Second Generation

2. Joseph Odlin (Joseph) was born about 1761, was buried on 21 Apr 1794 in Tetford, Lincolnshire.

Joseph was employed as Labourer.

Joseph married[4] **Rebecca Cosear** on 10 Aug 1784 in Tetford, Lincolnshire.

They had the following children:

     3 M   i. **William Odlin** was born about 1785 and died on 3 Mar 1867.

     4 M   ii. **John Odlin** was born about 1787 and was christened[5] on 18 Feb 1787 in Tetford, Lincolnshire.

Third Generation

William Odlin (Joseph, Joseph) was born about 1785 in Tetford, Lincolnshire and was christened[6] on 8 Jul 1785 in Tetford, Lincolnshire. He died[7] on 3 Mar 1867 in Tetford, Lincolnshire and was buried[8] on 7 Mar 1867 in Tetford, Lincolnshire.

William was employed as Farmer.

William married[9] **Mary Griffin**, daughter of John Griffin and Elizabeth ?, on 18 Jan 1810 in Tetford, Lincolnshire. Mary was born about 1791 in Tetford, Lincolnshire and was christened[10] on 7 Jul 1791 in Tetford, Lincolnshire. She died[11] on 29 Jul 1867 and was buried[12] on 1 Aug 1867 in Tetford, Lincolnshire.

They had the following children:

     5 M   i. **John Odlin** was born[13] on 4 May 1810 in Tetford, Lincolnshire and was christened[14] on 11 May 1810 in Tetford, Lincolnshire. He died[15] on 23 Mar 1882 in Tetford, Lincolnshire and was buried in Tetford, Lincolnshire.

                 John was employed as Farmer.

     6 M   ii. **William Odlin** was born on 4 Mar 1812 in Tetford, Lincolnshire and was christened[16] on 31 Mar 1812 in Tetford, Lincolnshire. He died[17] before 1860.

     7 F   iii. **Elizabeth Odlin** was born about 1814 in Tetford, Lincolnshire and was christened[18] on 6 Dec 1814 in Tetford, Lincolnshire. She died[19] on 5 May 1854

in Tetford, Lincolnshire and ...
Lincolnshire.

Elizabeth was employed as House Servant.

8 F   iv. Rebecca Odlin was born about 1817 and was christened[21] on 10 Feb 1817 in Tetford, Lincolnshire. *Date of ̶d̶e̶a̶t̶h̶ not known*

9 F   v. Mary Odlin was born about 1823 and was christened[22] on 18 May 1823 in Tetford, Lincolnshire. *Date of death not known*
Mary married **Robert Gilbert**, son of George Gilbert and Sarah ?. Robert was born[23] about 1822 in Saltfleetby St Peter, Lincolnshire and was christened[24] on 29 Apr 1822 in Saltfleetby St Peter, Lincolnshire. *Date of death not known*

Robert was employed as Cottager.

10 M   vi. **Joseph Odlin** was born about 1826 in Tetford, Lincolnshire. He died[25] on 8 Nov 1875 in Tetford, Lincolnshire and was buried in Tetford, Lincolnshire.

Joseph was employed as Farmers son.
Joseph married **Lucy ?**. Lucy was born[26] about 1827 in Bardney, Lincolnshire. She died[27] on 19 Jun 1877 and was buried in Tetford, Lincolnshire.

11 F   vii. **Eliza Odlin** was born about 1828 *in Tetford, Lincolnshire. Christened in Tetford on 4 May 1828*

12 F   viii. **Emily Odlin** was born about 1832 in Tetford, Lincolnshire and was christened[28] on 9 Jul 1837 in Tetford, Lincolnshire.

Emily was employed as Farmer.
Emily married **Edward Shadford**, son of James Shadford and Jane Hancock, on 31 Mar 1885 in Horncastle, Lincolnshire. Edward was born about 1817 in Tetford, Lincolnshire and was christened[29] on 14 Apr 1817 in Tetford, Lincolnshire. *Date of death not known*

13 M   ix. **Edward Odlin** was born about 1833 and died on 8 Nov 1907.

Fourth Generation

11. **Eliza Odlin** (William, Joseph, Joseph) was born about 1828 in Tetford, Lincolnshire and was christened[30] on 4 May 1828 in Tetford, Lincolnshire. *Date of death not known*

Eliza was employed as House Servant.

Eliza married **George Harrison**. George was born[31] about 1828 in Louth, Lincolnshire. *Date of death not known*

George was employed as Blacksmith, farmer.

They had the following children:

14 M   i. **George Harrison** was born[32] about 1856 in Tetford, Lincolnshire.

15 F   ii. **Elizabeth Ann Harrison** was born[33] about 1860 in Tetford, Lincolnshire.

16 F   iii. **Mary Harrison** was born[34] about 1866 in Tetford, Lincolnshire.

17 M   iv. **William Harrison** was born[35] about 1869 in Tetford, Lincolnshire.

13. **Edward Odlin** (William, Joseph, Joseph) was born about 1833 in Tetford, Lincolnshire and was christened[36] on 10 Sep 1833 in Tetford, Lincolnshire. He died[37] on 8 Nov 1907 in Swaby, Lincolnshire and was buried[38] on 11 Nov 1907 in Swaby, Lincolnshire.

Edward was employed as Cottager.

Edward married[39] **Emma Dickinson**, daughter of Robert Dickinson and Mary Goy, on 26 Jun

1856 in Farforth, Lincolnshire. Emma was born~~ on 17 Sep 1857 in Belchford, Lincolnshire and was christened[41] on 4 Jan 1846 in Belchford, Lincolnshire. She died[42] on 1 May 1908 in Swaby, Lincolnshire and was buried[43] on 4 May 1908 in Swaby, Lincolnshire.

Emma was employed as Servant.

They had the following children:

18 M   i.   **William Odlin** was born on 26 Aug 1856 and died on 7 Sep 1931. ✗

19 M   ii.   **Edward Odlin** was born[44] on 27 Oct 1859 in New Bolingbroke, Lincolnshire. He died about 1928.

        Edward was employed as Labourer.

20 F   iii.   **Mary Ann Odlin** was born on 27 Oct 1863. ∅ *date of death not to...*

21 M   iv.   **John Odlin** was born on 10 Nov 1865 and died on 21 Oct 1904. *- See No. 21*

22 M   v.   **Joseph Odlin** was born on 30 Apr 1868 and died on 9 Feb 1929. *- See No. 22*

23 M   vi.   **Robert Odlin** was born[45] on 11 Jan 1871 in Swaby, Lincolnshire and was christened[46] on 11 Feb 1877 in Swaby, Lincolnshire. He died on 15 Feb 1959 and was buried in Swaby, Lincolnshire.

        Robert was employed as Farmer.

24 M   vii.   **George Odlin** was born on 13 May 1873 and died about 1959. ◻ *No 24*

25 M   viii.   **Arthur Odlin** was born on 1 Feb 1876 and died on 21 Feb 1957. *See No 25*

26 M   ix.   **Frederic Odlin** was born on 10 Jun 1878 and died on 28 Mar 1969.

27 M   x.   **Ernest Odlin** was born[47] on 18 Dec 1880 in Swaby, Lincolnshire and was christened[48] on 25 Mar 1883 in Swaby, Lincolnshire. He died[49] on 16 May 1965 in Louth, Lincolnshire and was buried in Swaby, Lincolnshire.

        Ernest was employed as Grocer. *PITCHETT*
        Ernest married **Sarah Ann ?.** Sarah was born about 1862. She died in 1948 in Swaby, Lincolnshire and was buried in 1948 in Swaby, Lincolnshire.

Fifth Generation

18. **William Odlin** (Edward, William, Joseph, Joseph) was born[50] on 26 Aug 1856 in Farforth, Lincolnshire. He died on 7 Sep 1931.

William married **Selina ?.** Selina died after 1931. *date of birth not known*

They had the following children:

28 M   i.   **Thomas Edward Odlin.**

20. **Mary Ann Odlin** (Edward, William, Joseph, Joseph) was born[51] on 27 Oct 1863 in Revesby, Lincolnshire and was christened[52] on 22 Nov 1863 in Revesby, Lincolnshire.

Mary was employed as Domestic Servant. *on 14 May 1885*

Mary married **Edward Richard Kirkby,** son of William Kirkby and Maria ?. Edward was born about 1858 and was christened[53] on 16 Apr 1858 in Swaby, Lincolnshire.

Edward was employed as Labourer.

They had the following children: *(prior to her mother's marriage)*

29 F   i.   **Harriett Odlin** was born[54] on 13 Jul 1883 in Swaby, Lincolnshire and was

christened[22] on 30 Mar 1884 in Swaby, Lincolnshire. She died[26] on 1 Mar 1982 in Louth, Lincolnshire and was buried in Swaby, Lincolnshire.

Harriett was employed as Housekeeper.

21. **John Odlin** (Edward, William, Joseph, Joseph) was born[57] on 10 Nov 1865 in Tetford, Lincolnshire. He died[58] on 21 Oct 1904 in Swaby, Lincolnshire and was buried[59] on 23 Oct 1904 in Swaby, Lincolnshire.

John was employed as Labourer.

John married[60] **Charlotte Ann Robinson**, daughter of Charles Robinson and Mary Stocks, on 28 Mar 1901 in Swaby, Lincolnshire. Charlotte was born[61] on 4 Jul 1865 in Swaby, Lincolnshire and was christened[62] on 30 Jul 1865 in Swaby, Lincolnshire. She died[63] on 5 Mar 1902 in Swaby, Lincolnshire and was buried[64] on 9 Mar 1902 in Swaby, Lincolnshire.

They had the following children:

   30 M   i. **Charles Sydney Odlin** was born on 12 Feb 1902 and died on 9 Apr 1988.

22. **Joseph Odlin** (Edward, William, Joseph, Joseph) was born[65] on 30 Apr 1868 in Tetford, Lincolnshire. He died[66] on 9 Feb 1929 in Great Carlton, Lincolnshire and was buried in Great Carlton, Lincolnshire.

Joseph was employed as Farmer.

Joseph married[67] **Ada May Hoodlass**, daughter of James Hoodlass, on 30 Mar 1897 in Burwell, Lincolnshire. Ada was born about 1871. She died[68] on 30 Apr 1919 and was buried in Great Carlton, Lincolnshire. *see Page 6A*

They had the following children: *(Major Jim Odlin)*

   31 M   i. **James Edward Odlin** was born on 12 Dec 1897 and died on 23 Oct 1981.

   32 M   ii. **Frederick William Odlin** died after 1975. *Wife Alice gone South...* *Daughter Jean born 30 (now Mrs.)*

   33 F   iii. **Agnes Odlin.** *died in childbirth*
                 Agnes married **William Thomas Larder**. William was born about 1890. He died on 21 Apr 1967 and was buried in Saltfleetby St Peter, Lincolnshire.

   34 F   iv. **Edith May Odlin** was born[69] on 20 Apr 1903. She died on 30 Jul 1975 and was buried in Saltfleetby St Peter, Lincolnshire. *Edith was Agnes sister.*
                 Edith married **William Thomas Larder**. William was born about 1890. He died on 21 Apr 1967 and was buried in Saltfleetby St Peter, Lincolnshire. *No child*

   35 M   v. **Ernest Odlin** was born on 26 Nov 1908 and died on 13 Jul 1994.

   36 M   vi. **Jack Odlin** was born about 1913. He died[70] on 10 Nov 1945 in Germany and was buried in Great Carlton, Lincolnshire. *Jack Odlin was in the a... when he died*

24. **George Odlin** (Edward, William, Joseph, Joseph) was born[71] on 13 May 1873 in Swaby, Lincolnshire and was christened[72] on 11 Feb 1877 in Swaby, Lincolnshire. He died about 1959 in Ketsby, Lincolnshire and was buried in Swaby, Lincolnshire.

George was employed as Labourer.

George married[73] **Mary Smalley**, daughter of Thomas Smalley and Adelaide ?, on 20 Oct 1897 in Swaby, Lincolnshire. Mary was born[74] about 1873 in Thurlby, Lincolnshire.

They had the following children:

   37 M   i. **George Odlin** was born about 1898 and was christened[75] on 26 Jun 1898 in Swaby, Lincolnshire.
                 George married **Ivy Winfield**. *No children*

	38 F	ii.	**May Odlin** was born about 1900.
	39 F	iii.	**Evelyn Adelaide Odlin** was born about 1902. *(presumed Twins)*
	40 M	iv.	**Thomas Edward Odlin** was born about 1902.
	41 F	v.	**Alice Emma Odlin** was born about 1904.
	42 F	vi.	**Mary Odlin** was born about 1908 and was christened[76] on 12 Apr 1908 in Swaby, Lincolnshire. Mary married **Harold Borrill**.
	43 M	vii.	**Horace Odlin** was born about 1910 and was christened[77] on 17 Jul 1910 in Swaby, Lincolnshire. He died about 1928.
	44 F	viii.	**Annie Odlin** was born about 1911 and was christened[78] on 7 May 1911 in Swaby, Lincolnshire. She died about 1912 and was buried[79] on 30 Jul 1912 in Swaby, Lincolnshire.
	45 F	ix.	*22.10.1916* **Miriam Odlin** was born about 1917 and was christened[80] on 25 Feb 1917 in Swaby, Lincolnshire. Miriam married **Albert Brader**.

25. **Arthur Odlin** (Edward, William, Joseph, Joseph) was born[81] on 1 Feb 1876 in Swaby, Lincolnshire and was christened[82] on 11 Feb 1877 in Swaby, Lincolnshire. He died[83] on 21 Feb 1957 and was buried in Halton Holegate, Lincolnshire.

Arthur was employed as Farmer.

Arthur married[84] Eve Epton, daughter of William Epton and Elizabeth ?, on 6 May 1896 in Driby, Lincolnshire. Eve was born[85] on 3 Dec 1864 in South Thoresby, Lincolnshire. She died on 21 Apr 1958 and was buried on 24 Apr 1958 in Halton Holegate, Lincolnshire.

They had the following children:

	46 M	i.	**John Odlin** was born[86] on 13 Jan 1897 in Calceby, Lincolnshire and was christened[87] on 7 Mar 1897 in Driby, Lincolnshire. He died after 1956 and was buried in Burgh-le-Marsh, Lincolnshire. John married (1) **Dorothy ?**. John also married (2) **Patricia Kennedy**. Patricia died about 1959.
	47 M	ii.	**William Edward Odlin** was born on 10 Feb 1899 and died on 1 Jun 1982.
	48 M	iii.	**Albert Ernest Odlin** was born on 17 May 1901 and died on 8 Aug 1981.
	49 F	iv.	**Jessie June Odlin** was born on 29 Jun 1905 and died on 12 Jul 1993.
	50 M	v.	**Arthur Odlin** was born on 5 Oct 1906 and died on 24 Feb 1963.
	51 M	vi.	**Charlie Odlin** was born on 27 May 1908 and died on 29 Oct 1981.

Also Lily Elizabeth Epton (Illegitimate daughter of Eve Ep (see Page 5A)

26. **Frederic Odlin** (Edward, William, Joseph, Joseph) was born[88] on 10 Jun 1878 in Swaby, Lincolnshire and was christened[89] on 25 Mar 1883 in Swaby, Lincolnshire. He died on 28 Mar 1969 in Spilsby, Lincolnshire and was buried in Irby-in-the-Marsh, Lincolnshire.

Frederic married **Frances Jane Bunnage** on 15 May 1903 in Lusby, Lincolnshire. Frances was born on 28 Apr 1881 in Crowland, Lincolnshire. She died on 28 Oct 1962 in Spilsby, Lincolnshire and was buried in Irby-in-the-Marsh, Lincolnshire.

They had the following children:

	52 M	i.	**Thomas Edward Odlin** was born on 17 Feb 1904 and died on 17 Apr 1992.
	53 M	ii.	**Frederick Harwood Odlin** was born on 17 Oct 1905 and died on 23 Nov 1987.
	54 M	iii.	**Lewis Harold Odlin** was born on 30 Aug 1907 and died on 24 Feb 1989.